THE ARAB ECONOMY
PAST PERFORMANCE AND FUTURE PROSPECTS

A study prepared for
The Arab Bank Ltd.

THE ARAB ECONOMY
Past Performance and Future Prospects

YUSIF A. SAYIGH

OXFORD UNIVERSITY PRESS
1982

Oxford University Press, Walton Street, Oxford OX2 6DP
London Glasgow New York Toronto
Delhi Bombay Calcutta Madras Karachi
Kuala Lumpur Singapore Hong Kong Tokyo
Nairobi Dar es Salaam Cape Town
Melbourne Auckland
and associate companies in
Beirut Berlin Ibadan Mexico City

Published in the United States by
Oxford University Press, New York

British Library Cataloguing in Publication Data

Sayigh, Yusif A.
The Arab economy: past performance and future prospects.
1. Arab countries—Economic conditions
2. Arab countries—Economic policy
I. Title
330.917'4927 HC498
ISBN 0-19-877188-6

Typesetting by Hope Services, Abingdon
and printed in Great Britain by
Billing & Sons, Ltd., Guildford, London & Worcester

Foreword

On the occasion of its fiftieth anniversary, the Arab Bank requested Professor Yusif A. Sayigh to examine the record of economic development in the Arab region over the past fifty years, namely 1930–80, and to identify and assess the major issues which will influence the outlook for development in the remaining years of the century. The half-century considered has witnessed dramatic and far-reaching changes in Arab society and economy, and the Arab Bank is proud to have emerged as an important financial institution during the same time-span, and to have served the region's economy on a consistently expanding scale.

The present study was designed to address its two objectives – evaluating past development, and weighing the major issues in future development – briefly and in terms that the general reader would not find inhibiting. A much longer and more technical, academic work based on considerably more extensive research would have produced a more detailed and more rigorous study. However, on balance, it was thought that conciseness and greater readability were to be preferred, as they would bring the book to a much wider public.

The Bank wishes to thank Dr Sayigh warmly for his effort in preparing this book, and it trusts that the reader will find it a valuable addition to the library on the region's economy, particularly in view of the grave shortage of works with a broad Arab perspective.

ABDUL MAJEED SHOMAN
Chairman
Arab Bank Limited

28 February 1981

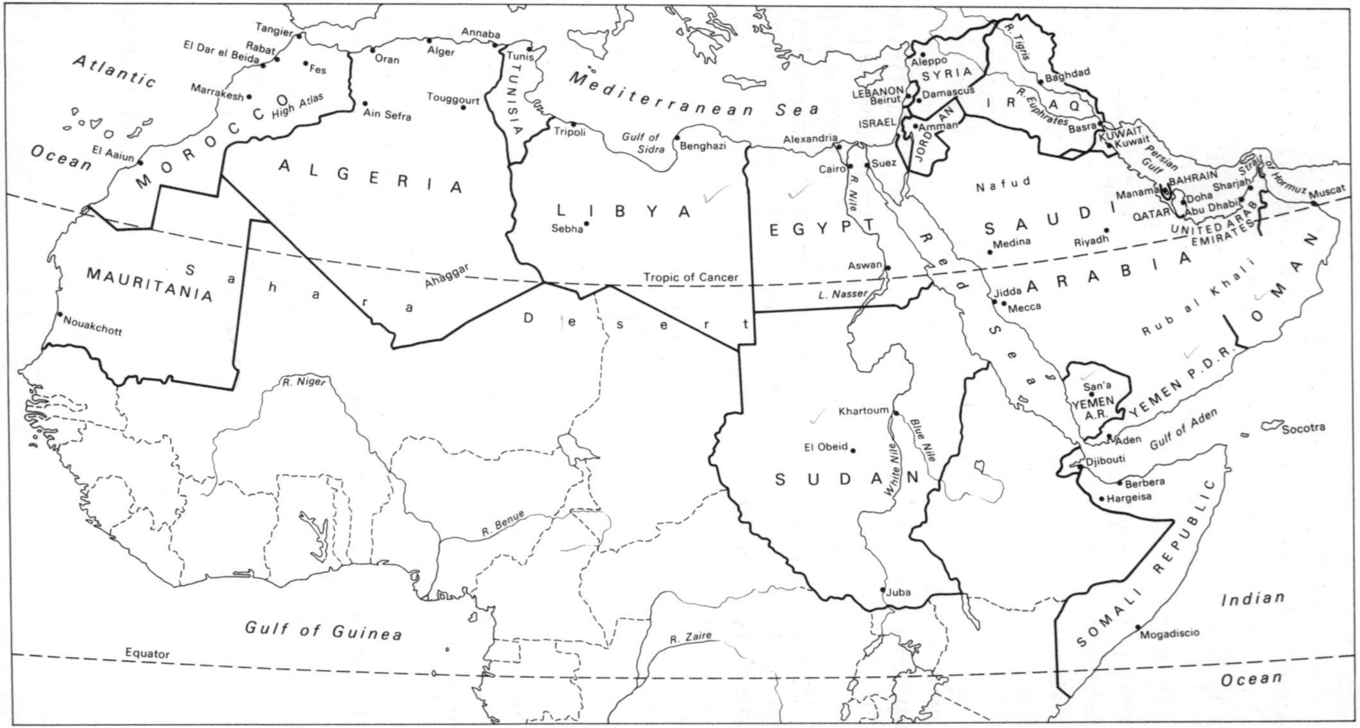

Atlantic Ocean
Tangier
Rabat
El Dar el Beida
Fes
Marrakesh
High Atlas
MOROCCO
El Aaiun
Oran
Alger
Annaba
Tunis
TUNISIA
Ain Sefra
Touggourt
ALGERIA
Mediterranean Sea
Tripoli
Gulf of Sidra
Benghazi
LIBYA
Sebha
MAURITANIA
Nouakchott
Sahara Desert
Ahaggar
Tropic of Cancer
Alexandria
Cairo
Suez
R. Nile
EGYPT
Aswan
L. Nasser
LEBANON
Beirut
ISRAEL
Aleppo
SYRIA
Damascus
Amman
JORDAN
R. Tigris
Baghdad
R. Euphrates
IRAQ
Basra
KUWAIT
Kuwait
Persian Gulf
Nafud
SAUDI ARABIA
Medina
Riyadh
Jidda
Mecca
Red Sea
Manama
BAHRAIN
QATAR
Doha
Sharjah
Abu Dhabi
UNITED ARAB EMIRATES
Strait of Hormuz
Muscat
Rub al Khali
OMAN
San'a
YEMEN A.R.
YEMEN P.D.R.
Aden
Gulf of Aden
Socotra
Djibouti
Berbera
Hargeisa
SOMALI REPUBLIC
Mogadiscio
Indian Ocean
Khartoum
Blue Nile
White Nile
El Obeid
SUDAN
Juba
R. Niger
R. Benue
R. Zaire
Gulf of Guinea
Equator

Preface

This book sets out to assess the change that has taken place in the economy of the Arab region, stretching from Iraq east to Morocco west, during the half-century 1930–80. The legitimacy of the treatment of the economies of the twenty-one sovereign states of which the region is composed as one regional economy, as the title of the book indicates, may be questioned if not denied outright. The argument might be put forth that there is no such thing as an 'Arab economy', and that it is both artificial and unacceptable to aggregate data relating to the individual economies and to consider the totals as representing an account of one regional economy. Admittedly, there would be a point to such criticism.

However, the artificiality of the political fragmentation itself must not be overlooked. This fragmentation was largely brought about by Western colonialism; it continues to exist, although political independence has been achieved, because of persistent interference by external forces and the pressure of certain internal vested interests associated with these forces. This network of interests feeds, and flourishes on fragmentation, and serves the purposes of the existing international economic order, the strength of which requires the weakness of peripheral underdeveloped economies. The Arab economy suffers more from fragmentation than it does from any other debilitating factor.

Yet in spite of this factor, there is a real and growing economic circuit of life in the Arab region, which flows through the areas of complementarity achieved among the national (i.e. individual) economies and through a joint sector. This sector has come into being and is being expanded mainly by deliberate national will and design, but it leaps across national frontiers to attain a regional reach. While it has not become a determining integrative force among the Arab economies and has not the same strength and spread of the economic exchanges and the interlocking that the Omayyad or Abbasid eras in Arab history witnessed, nevertheless the joint sector is a reality to contend with.

Since the independence of most parts of the Arab region after the Second World War, and the formation of the League of Arab States, many components of an institutional framework for Arab economic complementarity have been formally forged. To these have been added private efforts by several business and professional communities to establish intra-regional projects and associations. And the process has intensified since the adjustment of oil prices in 1973/4 and the increased flow of oil revenue into the region, with considerable financial and manpower flows across national frontiers. A few indicators will be sufficient to suggest the magnitude and reach of the joint economic sector.

In addition to the formation of many ministerial councils to serve co-ordinative, advisory, or operational purposes, and of many more intra-regional bodies at lower levels, scores of large joint projects with an aggregate capital of about $23 billion* have been established. Current official financial flows, mainly from the oil-exporting to the other countries, average about $5 billion of aid annually. A workforce of more than three million strong are employed in countries other than their own and send remittances back home of $3–4 billion every year. Finally, tens of thousands of students attend universities in Arab countries not their own. In financial terms alone, the aggregate capital of the joint economic sector (including development funds) exceeds $40 billion. But the significance of the sector goes beyond the size of its capital. It lies in the large and growing degree of sharing of burdens, capabilities, and resources.

Yet the sharing can, and should be, expanded considerably if the sector is to reach substantial dimensions, and if closer complementarity is to be achieved among significant parts of the Arab economies, for the promotion of development, welfare, and security – both for individual countries and for the region as a whole. The appreciation of this necessity has recently been endorsed at the highest political level, with the unanimous approval by the Arab Heads of State (at the Eleventh Summit held in Jordan in November 1980) of the 'Strategy for Joint Arab Economic Action' and the 'Charter

*One billion equals a thousand millions.

of National [i.e. Regional], Economic Action'. These two documents are currently being translated into a plan and action programmes, to provide a promotive framework and operational scope for greater complementarity and a more substantial joint sector. The financial and manpower resources required are available and promise to flow in abundance. Thus a robust and expanding Arab economy is in the making, alongside and in harmony with the national economies. It still needs a great deal of tending, but its promise is considerable.

Y. A. S.

Contents

1. Introduction

In the year 1930, which marks the opening of the half-century that is at the centre of our attention in Part One of this book, only two Arab countries were independent – Saudi Arabia and its southern neighbour, Yemen (now Arab Republic of Yemen).* A combination of factors had enabled them to acquire and maintain their independence ahead of the other Arab countries, but they belonged, paradoxically, to the distinctly less-developed group of Arab countries, rather than to the group of Arab countries which were relatively more advanced economically and socially. (The latter group comprised the three Maghreb countries under French occupation, namely Morocco, Algeria, and Tunisia, plus Egypt, Palestine, Lebanon, Syria, and Iraq.)

For many reasons, it is virtually impossible to make a detailed comparison of the Arab region as it stands today with its counterpart of fifty years ago. One reason is the changes that have occurred in the composition of what is today accepted as the 'Arab region'. It now includes three entities which were not normally listed as Arab in the early 1930s: Djibouti, Somalia, and Mauritania. Furthermore, a few Arab countries were fragmented in the 1930s and the fragments came under the hegemony of different European powers; in some instances the fragments within a country were regarded as autonomous although they all fell under the same foreign power. And Palestine, which – though under occupation – had all its population inside its borders, now has half this population in forced exile and is not, politically, an independent Arab state like the other Arab entities. Consequently, economic and social information on the twenty-

*Currently, twenty-one independent Arab states lie between the Arabian Gulf in the east and the Atlantic Ocean in the west: Iraq, Kuwait, Saudi Arabia, the United Arab Emirates, Bahrain, Qatar, Oman, the Arab Republic of Yemen, the People's Democratic Republic of Yemen, Jordan, Syria, Lebanon, Egypt, Sudan, Libya, Tunisia, Algeria, Morocco, Mauritania, Somalia, and Djibouti. Palestine, at the heart of the Arab region, has been under Zionist occupation since the establishment of Israel on Palestinian soil in 1948.

one Arab states of today cannot be matched by information for 1930.

The Arab countries as a whole had for centuries, after the emergence of Islam as a dynamic world religion, carved for themselves a prominent political position in the world, and had made notable scientific and cultural contributions to the heritage of man. But the twentieth century found them under foreign domination and in a state of cultural and economic dormancy and backwardness, compared with their distinguished past. The First World War, which had aroused hopes of national resurgence, brought in its wake a large measure of frustration. The Ottoman hegemony, which in many parts of the Arab region was only nominal, receded completely upon the military defeat of the Ottomans. Instead the region came under various forms of European control, except for those countries already ruled by European powers, and Saudi Arabia and Yemen, which escaped this fate. In two instances, Algeria and Palestine, the colonization was of a special brand: settler colonialism, which aimed at taking over the country entirely. As events were to show, the national population of Palestine was uprooted to make room for the settler colonialists who had been protected and supported by Western powers. But Algeria won its independence in 1962, after a long and costly war of liberation.

The protracted state of political submission to external power left deep marks on the cultural life of the Arab region and on its economic performance alike. Both were subdued and conditioned in order to serve the interests of the ruling powers and to weaken the tendency towards national resurgence and development. But, while under the Ottomans there was relatively intensive intra-regional trade and easy movement of persons, particularly in the Mashreq (that is, Egypt and the Asian Arab countries), under modern European rule both production and trade were directed in such a way that they became closely linked with Western Europe, and the erection of political frontiers restricted the movement of goods and travellers. The same reorientation occurred also in the cultural field. By 1930 most of the countries of the region were beginning to base their educational systems and cultural life generally on the Western model as they saw it. Modernization, which emerged as a strong driving force after the First World War, meant (and still means) westernization to virtually all political decision-makers, technocrats, thinkers, and opinion-makers.

It is necessary to emphasize the strong appeal of the 'western way of life' which ran parallel with the intensified contact with the West, in spite of the forced incursion of direct Western power into those countries it had not penetrated hitherto. This appeal in part explains the adoption of Western political forms of government and organization that was to be seen, in one country after another, in the era of independence after the Second World War. In the same way Western influences and interests combined to shape the socio-economic systems that were to be adopted consciously and deliberately, or to evolve gradually, unchallenged by any other system until the early 1960s. Hence a strange phenomenon came into view, during the fifty years under survey, whereby resentment against Western power and interests, leading often to political and/or armed resistance, existed side by side (particularly among the *élite* groups) with a desire to adopt the Western economic model, certain Western cultural values and attitudes, and a part of the life-style of the colonizing West.

If we narrow the focus to concentrate on economic life, we observe that the year 1930 was a rather significant landmark in the recent economic history both of the world at large and of the Arab region in particular. It represented the start of the era of the Great Depression of the advanced industrial countries, immediately after the 'Crash' of the autumn of 1929. The repercussions of the Depression, which lasted into the late 1930s and were to be largely absorbed by the preparations for the Second World War, spilled over into the less-developed countries – what we now call the developing countries of the Third World.

The spill-over took at least two major forms. The first was the spread of depression into Third World regions because purchases of raw materials from these regions declined under the strong downward pull of the Depression, and investment by the industrial countries in developing countries declined considerably.[1] The second form was the resultant slowing-down by Third World regions of purchases of manufactured goods – both capital and consumer goods – upon the shrinkage of their purchasing power and of foreign investment. The Great Depression also meant that the Western European countries, which were then by far the most important trading partners of the Arab world (the United States was not yet in the prominent position it was to attain in later decades), were too weak economically, and too busy with their own recovery, to exert as much economic pressure on the Arab countries under their political and/or economic hegemony as in the preceding decade.[2]

Fortuitously, the relative economic weakening of the advanced Western economies provided the opportunity for the less sluggish Arab economies to step up their own efforts to develop, with some increased investment in local industry under new protective policies. (The same thing was to happen again in a number of countries during the Second World War.) But such modest and spotty acceleration in developmental efforts as occurred at the start of the decade of the thirties was of very limited effect. There were no major active factors of sufficient and enduring impact to bring about radical transformation in the Arab economies. Thus, with the notable exception of Egypt, where Misr Bank (founded in 1920) took a relatively strong initiative in financing investment in industry and some other activities, the economies of the Arab world did not benefit spectacularly during the Depression from the relaxation of the grip of Western economic power. Yet it must be pointed out that the favourable impact of the relaxation, modest as it was, came to be felt most in the Mashreq, particularly in Egypt, Syria, Lebanon, Iraq, and Palestine.

The major changes that differentiate today's Arab world from that of the early 1930s fall mainly in the post-independence era after the Second World War, and can be attributed primarily to the impact of independence on the national economies. A strong supplementary factor, though of more recent influence, is the vast expansion in the production and earnings of the hydrocarbon sector. Similarly, the great strides in education and manpower training, and in the establishment of some of the institutions and infrastructure of modern societies, were made only in the immediate postwar period or even in the last two or three decades.

A detailed, analytical survey of developments in the Arab economies over the period 1930–80 is not possible for several reasons. First and foremost is that already referred to with respect to the non-comparability of the political entities that form the Arab region at the two terminal dates. To this must be added the unavailability of a large body of essential data, and the spottiness of the data available, especially for the earliest years. This is true both of the various sectors involved and of the various countries. Furthermore, many developments, particularly those relating to joint Arab economic action and institutions, had no counterparts in the early 1930s, and any meaningful comparison is therefore impossible.

Lastly, a survey in detail and in depth would require much more research and space than the present brief study allows. An attempt will therefore be made in Part One of this book to examine first the major developments over the past fifty years in selected sectors and areas of activity, where some comparison is possible; and, secondly, to examine the overall economic performance of the region and the degree of co-operation and complementarity it has achieved. With this performance as background, Part Two will attempt to evaluate the prospect for development in the remaining years of the twentieth century by identifying the major issues and tasks that will be required if this development is to be profound and comprehensive, and therefore worthy of the efforts, resources, and hopes that the Arabs invest in it.

Before the reader goes any further towards examining the record of economic performance, he is warned to accept much of the quantitative information with a certain degree of judicious scepticism. The statistical services in the Arab region are mostly still in their formative stage, and the data they collect and publish do not always enjoy a high degree of reliability. The researcher has, nevertheless, to accept these data. It is the author's hope that he has been as careful as possible in the acceptance and use of the material available.

PART I

Major developments 1930–1980

2. Man, land, and water

In setting out to trace and evaluate the course of Arab economic development over the half-century 1930–80, it is appropriate to look first at the Arabs and their physical environment, because basically it is the man/land relationship that determines the survival of societies and their fundamental economic performance and well-being. By 'land' we mean the total physical environment. But in the present study the discussion will be restricted to land and water, the main factors in shaping rural/agricultural conditions – apart from the population.

The present chapter focuses on the relationship between the population and its land (and water) resources because of the pre-eminence of the rural sector and agricultural activity in the life of the Arab region. Thus, while the hydrocarbon sector has become the largest sector, with the emergence of oil and gas as the most vital resources, and while industry is potentially a significant sector, in terms of contribution to Gross Domestic Product and activation of the economy, in the 1930s and for many subsequent years it was agriculture that occupied the place of honour in the Arab economies. Even today the rural sector defined broadly is still the dominant reality in the Arab region; it maintains over half the aggregate population and provides employment and livelihood for about one-fourth to one-third of the region's labour supply. Furthermore, land and water are not merely the prerequisites for agricultural activities and the production of foodstuffs: they also influence the climate and the general character of a region, its institutions, and its social structure and culture.

The aggregate population of the Arab world including all the countries that *today* form part of this region (that is, the twenty-one sovereign states already listed, plus the Palestinian Arabs) is estimated (or recorded) by the League of Nations Economic Intelligence Service to have been some 53 million in 1930 or thereabouts (the data do not all relate

TABLE 1

Population of the Arab Countries, 1930/1 and 1979 (a)
(in thousands)

Country	1930/1	1979
Iraq	3,300	12,900
Arabia [b]	7,000	
Kuwait		1,283
Saudi Arabia		8,200
Bahrain	120	352
Qatar		212
UAE		761
Oman		872
Yeman A.R.		5,870
Aden–Perim [c]	51	
P.D.R. Yemen		1,920
Transjordan [d]	300	
Palestine [e]	1,040	
Jordan [f]		3,013
Syria [g]	2,800	8,470
Lebanon [g]		3,121
Egypt	14,920	41,400
Sudan	5,508	18,140
Libya	715	2,900
Tunisia	2,450	6,460
Algeria	6,650	19,400
Morocco [h]	6,562	19,750
Mauritania [i]	324	1,606
Somalia [j]	1,420	3,580
Djibouti		118
Total	53,160	160,328 (*k*)

Notes:

[a] Most of the figures for 1930 or 1931 are shown as estimates in the sources. Data for end 1979 are projections from published data for 1977 or 1978 in the sources indicated. The projection was made at the rates of increase immediately preceding 1979.

[b] 'Arabia' includes what is currently known as: Kuwait, United Arab Emirates, Qatar, Oman, Yemen Arab Republic, and People's Democratic Republic of Yemen (except Aden and Perim) as well as Saudi Arabia proper.

[c] 'Aden and Perim' now form part of P.D.R. Yemen.

[d] 'Transjordan' refers to what is now known as the East Bank of Jordan.

[e] The population of Palestine in 1930/1 included 174,606 Jews. The total number of Palestinians at end of 1979 was approximately 4,000,000, about half of whom were in Palestine (as defined under the British Mandate) and half in the diaspora which was created by the establishment of Israel in 1948.

[f] Jordan's population includes the West Bank (Palestine) as well as the East Bank. Roughly two-thirds of this population are of Palestinian origin.

[g] Syria and Lebanon were treated together in the source for 1930/1.

[h] The population of Morocco in 1930/1 included the various parts under the

to that year), while the aggregate is about 162 million for the end of 1979. The tripling of the Arabs in fifty years indicates a high rate of natural increase – about 2.2 per cent per annum on average (see Table 1).

The rate is actually very uneven among countries and over time, being much lower in the early years and much higher in the later years. Relatively reliable demographic data are avialable for only a few countries: Egypt, Palestine, and the Maghreb countries then under French rule. But enough is known in general terms to suggest that the rise in the natural rate of increase is due more to the drop in mortality over the years than to a rise in fertility. For the region as a whole, curative and preventive medicine, the spread of hygiene instruction, the advance in public health services, dietary improvements, and the lengthening of thc period of fertility have together rcsulted in lower mortality rates, higher fertility rates, and much higher rates of net increase.[3]

Some qualifications are necessary if the picture that emerges from the preceding paragraph is not to be misleading. First, despite the amelioration in health-care facilities and services, and the control of several endemic and epidemic diseases in many parts of the Arab region, modernization has, on the negative side, introduced some diseases that had earlier been of very limited incidence. Furthermore, the rapid crowding of urban centres and the emergence of slums on a large scale have checked the improvement, or even caused a deterioration, in the living conditions of many new urban dwellers compared with their earlier life in the countryside.

---

control of different European powers, as well as Tangier and the islands off the shore.

i No data are available in the source for 1930/1 or 1979 on the population of the Western Sahara.

j Djibouti is not shown as a separate political entity in the source for data related to 1930/1; it formed part of French Somalia then, and as such is included in the population estimate of 1,420,000.

k The total for end of 1979 should include the Palestinians not included in the table (some 2,000,000) as well as the population of the Western Sahara (see note *i*).

Sources: For 1930/1, League of Nations, *Statistical Yearbook of the League of Nations*, 1932/3 (Geneva 1933). For end of 1979 (except for Djibouti), *International Financial Statistics*, September 1980 (data projected to end of 1979); for Djibouti, FAO, *FAO Production Yearbook 1978*, Table 3.

A second and related qualification must be made in connection with diet: for many villagers the availability of food and the balance of diet were better assured in the earlier part of the period under examination than they are now that the villagers have moved to the cities and become urbanized. Finally, pollution, a much more recent phenomenon, is a problem in the Arab region as elsewhere.

These qualifications apart, living conditions for the mass of the aggregate population of the Arab world are distinctly better today, though the scope for improvement is still enormous. This statement is particularly relevant to the poorer strata of the population in each of the countries, and to those who are more distant from towns and cities and therefore from health-care facilities and services. The tendency for these services to be concentrated in the cities is a common phenomenon, in spite of efforts by many governments to spread the facilities and services more evenly. Even the public health-care systems, which are purportedly guided by social conscience rather than the motive of private profit, which is operative in the case of private doctors and hospitals, are markedly inadequate in the countryside, and this becomes more obvious the further away the villages are from the capitals and district centres. Moreover, in addition to the insufficiency of the services in terms of volume and distribution, there are qualitative deficiencies which are openly acknowledged in the region.

Nevertheless, the average Arab of today is healthier and better looked after in terms of health care, better informed of the dictates of hygiene, and has a higher life expectancy. Life expectancy at birth in 1978 (the last year for which data are available) stood at a low of 39 years at one extreme, but at 65 and 69 years respectively for Lebanon and Kuwait, at the other extreme, for the twenty countries covered by the data.* The two countries named are the only Arab countries enjoying a life expectancy that is higher than the weighted average for the group of countries to which they belong, according to the classification by the World Bank.[4]

No information of equal spread and credibility is available

*No data are available for Djibouti.

for 1930 or thereabouts. The only exception relates to Egypt, which, with Palestine and, to a lesser extent, the Maghreb countries of Morocco, Algeria, and Tunisia, had reasonably good vital statistics for those days. Life expectancy at birth in Egypt as calculated for the decade 1927–37 was about 31 years.[5] There are some very rough estimates for the other countries listed, but they are invariably heavily qualified, and there is little to be gained by quoting them. From general surveys of all the countries of the region it can be surmised that life expectancy was distinctly lower in the early thirties than it is today, especially for the countries which currently enjoy high or relatively high expectancy, such as Lebanon and Kuwait, as well as Morocco, Algeria, Tunisia, Libya, Syria, Iraq, and Jordan. (For all of these the figure is over 54 years, which was the life expectancy in 1978 for Egyptians.)

Change in life expectation over the past half-century is significant in itself, as indicator of man's widened opportunity, in terms of life span, to acquire the knowledge, skills, and experience that he needs both for his productive endeavours and for the enjoyment of the fruit of these endeavours. But life span is not sufficient in itself to enable man to benefit in this way: education and training, as well as social organization and work opportunities, are necessary.

Expanded life expectancy has influenced this dual role of man in three respects. First, in granting more years of active life, it has provided wider scope for education and training. This has been reflected in lengthened schooling and instruction. Secondly, it has allowed the attainment of greater experience and a longer period of gainful employment, during which the education and training acquired can be capitalized. Finally, it has influenced the age structure of the Arab population by raising the dependency ratio at both ends of the age scale. Thus, though the high birth-rates meant that a large proportion – probably a little under half the population – in the 1930s were below 20 years of age, only a very small percentage were above 65, which is generally considered the age for retirement. Today the age structure at the lower end of the scale differs from that in the thirties: roughly 55 per cent of the population are below 20 years of age. But there is much greater difference at the other end of the scale, with many more Arabs than ever before living beyond their fifties and sixties. The proportion of dependants of older age has therefore increased considerably over the years. The fact that this lays economic claims on society, in terms of services and care for the aged is counterbalanced by the lengthening of the period of active employment.

The tripling of the aggregate Arab population between 1930 and 1980 together with the widened life span of this population have impinged strongly on the natural resources of the region, though in different degrees in the various countries, depending mainly on the relative richness of the natural endowments of each. We shall not attempt to examine the relationship between population and all resources, but simply the man/land ratio broadly defined, that is, taking into account water resources as well.

It can be said straight away that in general the population has increased faster than the expansion in the land and water resources utilized and the intensification of their utilization. As far as land is concerned, the area reported has increased from 11.2 to 13.5 m.km^2.[6] In many of the countries this is due in part to boundary changes, but the chief cause of the variations is the tentativeness of the early land surveys.

These variations, however, are not as wide as those encountered in a comparison of specific categories of land between the early post-war years (mainly 1947 and 1948) and the later years. A note of explanation is called for at this point: data relating to much earlier dates, such as 1930, are available for some countries both in the Mashreq and in the Maghreb, but these are not comparable between countries like the recent data in hand. For the earlier data the researcher has to use country surveys, and these have not been subjected to any systematization or standardization at the regional level, as the data in FAO sources (which we use) have been. We have therefore opted for the earliest complete FAO data for 1947 or 1948, since they have been standardized and the same definitions of the various categories of land apply to them as to the most recent data relating to 1977. As the comparison will lead only to tentative and provisional conclusions, very little is lost in not referring back to much older sporadic country data. Furthermore, even in 1947 or 1948 information on cultivated land was not available for the whole of the Arabian Peninsula or for Libya and Mauritania; and estimates of cultivable land, which are nebulous at best and vary according to definitions and assumptions, are lacking for all except Syria and Sudan in the earliest FAO reference.[7]

Cultivated land is divided in FAO statistics into three categories: arable land and permanent crops (including temporary crops, temporary meadows for mowing or pasture, land under market and kitchen gardens, and land temporarily fallow or lying idle, as well as land under permanent crops); permanent meadows and pastures; and forests and woodland. All these categories of land appear in earlier and recent FAO source material alike. There is, however, no explicit mention of cultivable, or potentially productive, land in recent statistics; instead this category is lumped in with 'other land', which also includes built-on areas, wasteland, parks, roads, barren land, and any other types not listed in the first three categories. In earlier FAO statistics there is a category entitled 'unused but potentially productive' land; as already indicated, however, information regarding this category is available for only two countries.

This lengthy explanation is necessary in order to show why an interesting comparison cannot be made over time: namely between areas considered potentially cultivable some decades ago and those considered so today. Such a comparison would be of great value for an assessment of the agricultural potential of the region in view of its fast expanding need for agricultural produce. Current estimates of cultivable land can be found for individual countries in national sources, but these, as already indicated, cannot be compared owing to methodological differences. Nevertheless, they are useful for comparison with areas actually cultivated; they indicate, even if only tentatively, the gap between actual and potential cultivation. At present, however, such a comparison can be made for some of the region's countries only; comparison with earlier decades is not possible, as already stated, owing to the lack of data.

In examining progress in land use over the years, we shall therefore have to confine ourselves to two comparisons:

TABLE 2

Land use in Arab countries, 1947–77
(1000 ha)

Country	Total land area 1947/8	Total land area 1977	Cultivable area 1947/8	Cultivable area 1977	Arable and permanent crops 1947/8	Arable and permanent crops 1977	Permanent meadows and pastures 1947/8	Permanent meadows and pastures 1977	Woods and forests 1947/8	Woods and forests 1977	Irrigated areas 1977
Iraq	43,522	43,397		12,100	2,650*	5,290F	4,000*	4,000*	1,500*	1,500*	1,160F
Kuwait	2,072	1,782		3	n.a.	1	n.a.	134	n.a.	2	1
Saudi Arabia	154,500	214,969		1,500	20*	1,110F	n.a.	85,000*	n.a.	1,601*	390F
Bahrain	60	62		(5)	n.a.	2*	n.a.	4*	n.a.	n.a.	1*
Qatar	2,200	1,100		(5)	n.a.	2F	n.a.	50F	n.a.	n.a.	n.a.
UAE		8,360		(5)		11		200F		2F	5*
Oman	21,240	21,246		(5)	n.a.	36*	n.a.	1,000F	n.a.	n.a.	n.a.
Yemen A.R.	19,500	19,500		(5)	n.a.	1,570	n.a.	7,000	n.a.	1,600	230
P.D.R. Yemen	27,215	33,297		(5)	110	265*	n.a.	9,065*	n.a.	2,480F	58
Jordan	9,111	9,718		1,200	480	1,365F	600	100*	35	125*	60*
Syria	17,110	18,412		8,415	2,500	5,509	3,863	8,531	412	452	531F
Lebanon	1,017	1,023		330	239	348F	215	10*	80	76F	85F
Egypt	100,000	99,545		4,420	2,445	2,831F	–	–	–	2	2,831F
Sudan	250,583	237,600		45,000	717	7,495F	24,038	24,000F	94,100	91,500	1,550F
Libya	175,954	175,954		8,800	n.a.	2,544F	n.a.	6,750F	n.a.	534*	135F
Tunisia	15,583	15,536		5,000	3,766	4,410F	4,225	3,250*	1,009	520F	130F
Algeria	220,486	238,174		10,000	5,676	7,542	41,311	36,258*	3,000	4,122	285
Morocco	44,174	44,630		8,000	7,924	7,840F	7,700	12,500*	3,950	5,195F	470*
Mauritania		103,040		(5)		199	–	39,250*	–	15,134*	8

Somalia	69,936	62,734		(5)	7,997	1,066F	32,980	28,850*	2,700	8,650F	165F
Djibouti	2,200	2,198		(5)	2	1*	n.a.	244*	62	6*	n.a.
Total	1,176,463	1,352,277		104,768 4,000[5] 108,768	34,526	49,437	118,932	266,196	106,848	133,501	8,095

Notes:

1. Symbols: * = Unofficial figures (according to FAO sources listed below).
   F = FAO estimates.
   n.a. = Not available in source; no data mentioned.
   — = None or negligible; used in FAO *1950 Yearbook*, but not in *1978 Yearbook*.
2. Country definitions: Yemen Democratic Republic of today was designated 'Aden colony, including Perim and Kuria', and the Protectorate, in the FAO *1950 Yearbook*.
   French Somalia in *1950 Yearbook* is today's Djibouti.
   British Somalia and Somalia in *1950 Yearbook* together constitute today's Somalia; the latter does not, however, include the area of Ogadine which was considered part of Somalia in the forties. Hence the difference in land area between 1947 and 1977.
   Mauritania did not appear in *1950 Yearbook*.
   Spanish Morocco in *1950 Yearbook* does not appear in *1978 Yearbook*; it is today a disputed area touching on Mauritania, Morocco, and Algeria.
   Total area differences relate essentially to greater recent precision in land survey and boundary definition; in a few cases they relate to political adjustments.
3. No information is available in *1950 Yearbook* on area of irrigated land.
4. All areas given other than 'total land area' are tentative, as the notation with 'F' or asterisk suggests. Furthermore, irrigated area is greatly influenced by the definition used; thus, for Syria as illustration, the area was 579 (1961–5), 538 (1967), 625 (1972), and 531 (1977), dropping in 16 years in spite of expansion in irrigation facilities.
5. The aggregate area of 'cultivable land' for countries marked (5) is estimated at 4,000 in source (3) below.

Sources: (1) FAO, *Yearbook of Food and Agricultural Statistics 1950*, vol. IV, Part 1 (Washington D.C., 1951), Table 1.
(2) FAO, *1978 Production Yearbook* (Rome, 1979), Tables 1 and 2.
(3) Yusif A. Sayigh, *The Economies of the Arab World* (Croom Helm, London, 1978), p. 669 for 'cultivable area'.

that between areas in use in a limited number of countries for the late forties and the late seventies, and that between areas in use and areas capable of use[8] for most if not all countries in the late seventies (see Table 2). Some inferences will thereafter be drawn from this examination, though with the strong proviso that the data from which the inferences are gleaned, particularly those relating to 'cultivable areas', are no more than tentative and contain a large margin of error. Indeed, the wide variations in the areas reported as being cultivated in the seventies, a period that is so recent as to inspire confidence in the statistics, themselves indicate that even this type of statistical reporting is imprecise. A look at Table 2 confirms this, with virtually all data for 1977, other than total land area of the countries listed, being marked either as an unofficial estimate or one made by the FAO itself. (Data on 'cultivable land', as stated earlier, come from a large variety of non-FAO sources and can all be said to have an even more modest degree of reliability than data on actual land use.)

The first comparison to be undertaken here is that between 1947/8 and 1977 for arable land, that is, in FAO terminology, land actually cultivated. Double-cropped land, which constitutes a tiny proportion of total cultivated land, and which is of some importance only in Egypt, is counted only once. The comparison shows that expansion in cultivated area was 30 per cent by 1977, for those thirteen countries for which comparable information for 1947 or 1948 is available. The expansion becomes twice as large, that is 62 per cent, if we exclude Somalia and Saudi Arabia from the list of countries compared, because the steep drop in area cultivated in the one and the steep rise in the other make the record relating to them highly dubious. These adjustments apart, the change in area cultivated looks reasonable and justifiable for the other countries, the most notable expansion in relative terms having beeen recorded in Sudan, Jordan, People's Democratic Republic of Yemen, Syria, and Iraq. Sudan heads the list both in absolute and in relative terms.

If, however, we look at the areas involved, we find that they are not spectactular in absolute terms, even after taking the expansion into account. Thus, the area cultivated, according to Table 2 rose from 345,000 km^2 in 1947/8 to 450,000 km^2

(figures rounded) in 1977 if we take all thirteen countries into account, but from 265,000 to 429,000 if we drop Somalia and Saudi Arabia. In either case this is a very modest portion of the total land area of the countries concerned. (It constitutes just under 5 per cent of total land area for the thirteen countries, or just under 6 per cent for the eleven countries). However, compared with cultivable land as reported for the eleven countries, the proportion rises to 41 per cent.

It would probably be more instructive to refer to the man/land situation for the whole region, but this is possible only for 1977, as the data for 1947/8 have many gaps. None the less, it can be seen that for the thirteen (or even the eleven) countries, the land area cultivated expanded by distinctly less than the increase in population. The increase over the thirty years in question was not far from 150 per cent, against an expansion of merely 30 per cent for the thirteen countries (or 62 per cent for the eleven countries). The situation is no better for the region as a whole: indeed, it is arguably worse, since the countries excluded from the calculations are all ones in which the population has grown considerably, as in the group of thirteen countries, but where expansion in cultivated area has been distinctly slower, owing to the fact that all the countries excluded, except Libya and Mauritania, are in the Arabian Gulf where agricultural land is negligible.

Furthermore, for the region as a whole, as for the group of thirteen, there can be no great expectations from the cultivable rather than the cultivated land. The latter category already constitutes some two-fifths of the former, which suggests the close limits for horizontal expansion for a population of a size which has already far outdistanced expansion over the past fifty years, and which still increases at about 2.6 to 2.8 per cent per annum. As things stand today, a population of some 162 million has to find its food and other agricultural produce in a mere 495,000 km^2. This represents a high pressure on land resources, amounting to 327 persons per square kilometre (or 3.27 persons per hectare). Even granting that only about 55 per cent of this aggregate population lives in the rural sector, which seems to reduce the pressure by about half, it still remains high if we take into account the fact that this cultivated area must provide for the whole population, not just the rural population.

This leads us to the question of irrigation and whether by means of intensification of agriculture, it has been instrumental in reducing the pressure on the land resources. Here again redress escapes the Arab economies: the total area under irrigation in 1977 was no more than some 81,000 km^2, or 16.4 per cent of the area under cultivation (but a mere 7.4 per cent of estimated cultivable area, or an insignificant proportion of total land area – 0.6 per cent).

The area under irrigation is, however, no true guide to the availability of water in the region. Rainfall on the whole is adequate only in small scattered parts of the region and is, furthermore, seasonal and undependable. Rivers are limited in number and concentrated mainly in Iraq, Sudan, Egypt, and Syria (with smaller rivers in Lebanon, Jordan, and Morocco). There is, moreover, a general inefficiency in the harnessing and use of water resources. Considerable waste is prevalent not only in the failure to catch the waters of torrential rains, or to utilize all river and wadi water, but also in the failure to make proper and most economic use of the water that is harnessed for irrigation and for industrial and household purposes. According to a well-known Arab authority on the subject, 'The volume of water used for irrigation purposes in ECWA countries (that is, Egypt and the Asian Arab countries) is estimated at 80–90 billion m^3/year. The potential water resources available for agriculture are estimated at about 140 billion m^3.'[9] Furthermore, the investments and efforts put into the expansion of irrigation dams and networks are to a considerable extent neutralized through the failure to provide parallel facilities for drainage. The imbalance has proved both costly and damaging in all cases.

Yet, grim as the general account of water availability and use is, it still represents a vast improvement in the harnessing of water resources over the past fifty years. This improvement has been registered in the countries cited above, as well as in Algeria, Tunisia, and Saudi Arabia, mainly through the construction of dams and barrages across rivers, catchments to hold and store the water of seasonal wadis and floods, and irrigation systems. By 1930 the region had only a few large dams: specifically in Sudan, Egypt, and Iraq, as Table 3 shows.[10]

TABLE 3

Major dams in 1930

Country	Dams and barrages (a)	Year built (extension by 1930 or thereabouts)	Capacity by 1930 or thereabouts
Egypt	Aswan	1902, 1907–10, 1932–4	5.7 bn. m^3
	Esna	1908	
	Nag' Hammadi	1930	
	Assiut	1902	
Sudan	Sennar (b)	1925	3.5 bn. m^3
	Gabal al-Awlia (c)	1937	3.5 bn. m^3
Iraq	Hindiyyah	1913	
	Kut	1929	

Notes:

(a) Only major barrages are listed.

(b) Only 922 million cubic metres of the capacity indicated were for the use of Sudan, according to an agreement with Egypt in 1929.

(c) A limit of only 1 billion cubic metres was set for the use of Sudan.

By contrast, in 1980 many large dams and barrages were in existence, the most notable being the High Dam in Egypt, the Euphrates dam in Syria, the Samarra, Dokan, Derbendi Khan, and Habbaniyyah dams in Iraq, and the Roseires and Khashm el-Girba dams in Sudan. The gross aggregate storage capacity of these dams exceeds 110 bn. m^3.[11] (Seepage and evaporation must be accounted for.) This figure excludes regulators, subsidiary barrages, and diversion lakes (as in the case of Iraq), and the dams built by the end of the 1970s in Morocco, Tunisia, Jordan, Saudi Arabia, and Lebanon. Storage and control capacity for the region as a whole, not just the countries singled out, is now over five times what it was in 1930. Yet, significant though the expansion in useful storage capacity has been, it is not matched by as impressive an expansion in productive capacity in agriculture. This is because the area of land benefiting from irrigation is still modest compared with total cultivable area, as we showed earlier.

A notable by-product of the more recent construction of dams has been the vast expansion in the generation of electricity. Reliable information on hydroelectric generating capacity in the early thirties is not, however, available to show the extent of growth in this field. It is worth noting that most of the output of electricity in Egypt in the late thirties was thermal, and it was some 288 m. kWh annually; by the late 1970s it had risen to over 11,000 m. kWh annually, mostly hydraulic, thanks to the High Dam, the full capacity of which is set at 2,100 MW. The Euphrates dam in Syria together with the dams in Iraq have an installed capacity of 5,000 MW (capable of producing 50,000 m. kWh a year), to say nothing of the hydroelectric capacity in other countries. Virtually all hydroelectric capacity installed in the Arab world has come into being during the half-century under examination.

It is necessary at this point to return to the main concern of this chapter, namely population and land. As we have seen, the relative scarcity of cultivable and cultivated land, and of reliable sources of water in particular, constitute very serious problems for a satisfactory balance between population and land, and are enough in themselves to betray a very heavy population pressure on natural resources. But this is not all: these problems and handicaps 'are compounded by low labour productivity, backward farming techniques, inadequate investment in land and water resources, and the resulting low yields and small income of share-tenants and wage-farmers who constitute a large part of the rural population.'[12]

The rural sector has also suffered from an imbalance between itself and the urban sector, both broadly defined. Thus, over the past half-century, but particularly in the last three decades, there has been a large and growing movement towards urbanization. As is usual in all Third World regions, this has been caused by a combination of push and pull factors; and, as usual, the emigrants from the rural sector, many of whom are enterprising, ambitious, and socially mobile, have been considerably disappointed in what the urban sector has had to offer. They have mostly failed to find the jobs, housing, and education and health services which had lured them in the first place, and to earn the income with which to enjoy the attractions of the city.

At the same time, the countryside has failed to provide the financial and social rewards which were promised in policy statements and measures of agrarian reform and which could have supplied the motivation and the security necessary to arrest the demographic bleeding of the countryside.

Unfortunately, data on urbanization for the whole period under consideration are not available. Indeed, the FAO *Yearbook* of 1950, which was the first complete issue in the series, had no information on rural and urban population for any Arab country; such information was available for only three countries in the whole of Asia and Africa: Japan, Turkey, and the Union of South Africa.[13]

However, information on urbanization for very broad groupings of countries is available for the three decades beginning with 1950. Although this information does not show the Arab countries by themselves but includes them in the group of 'developing countries', it is none the less usable for our purposes, as it is the only comparison in hand which is based on a standardized definition of urbanization and applicable to all countries. Furthermore, detailed information on developing countries for the period 1960–75 suggests that the Arab region has not been behind other developing regions in the urbanization movement. Indeed some Arab cities rank among those Third World cities with the highest growth rates, and in most cases the degree of urbanization is higher than that for countries in the same income bracket. The developing countries have the highest average annual percentage growth of urban population for the period 1950–80, outdistanced only by Kuwait, Qatar, United Arab Emirates, Saudi Arabia, and Libya.[14] However, as these are also developing countries in the context of the present study, the statement about the high degree of urbanization in Third World countries is strengthened. Table 4 gives the change in fifteen years in the size of the urban population as percentage of total population in most Arab countries.

The structural shift in population in favour of urbanization can be seen most clearly in the growth of primate cities in the Arab world. The data available reveal the vast expansion in these cities in relation to both total and urban population in

TABLE 4

Urbanization in Arab countries 1960–75

Country	Urban population as percentage of total population 1960	1975
Iraq	43	66
Kuwait	72	84
Saudi Arabia	30	59
Bahrain	n.a.	40
Qatar	n.a.	85
UAE	n.a.	80
Oman	n.a.	5
Yemen A.R.	3	8
P.D.R. Yemen	28	34
Jordan	43	53
Syria	37	47
Lebanon	44	70
Egypt	38	44
Sudan	10	20
Libya	23	44
Tunisia	36	48
Algeria	30	54
Morocco	29	37
Mauritania	3	23
Somalia	17	27

Source: The World Bank, *World Development Report 1979*, Annex Table 20, pp. 164–5, and United Nations Economic Commission for Western Asia, *Demographic and Related Socio-Economic Data Sheets for Countries of The Economic Commission for Western Asia* (No. 2; Beirut 1978).

the vast majority of countries.[15] Behind the information that appears in Table 5 lies the story of a tough race between urban concentration and the provision of amenities for the growing population – one which the amenities never seem to win. The race is all the tougher currently; as the data in Tables 4 and 5 show, there is a marked progression in urban concentration in all but five countries.

On the surface, this shift of population from the rural sector to the urban centres suggests a welcome lightening of the pressure of population on natural resources – specifically, land and water in the present context. Reality, however, is different. In the first place, in 14 out of the 16 countries for which data are available for the nineteen years 1960–78, the absolute size of the active labour force engaged in agriculture has risen, although the proportion of this force in the total labour force has dropped in all but one country.[16] (In Libya and Lebanon both the absolute size and the proportion have dropped, while in Kuwait the proportion has risen. However, the proportion is tiny in this last case, reaching 1.7 per cent in 1978.) This development means that the labour–land mix has not been changed in a way that suggests any lightening of the population pressure on land resources.

TABLE 5

Concentration of urban population in large cities in Arab countries, 1960–75

Country	Percentage of urban population: in largest city 1960	in largest city 1975	in cities of over 500,000 inhabitants 1960	in cities of over 500,000 inhabitants 1975	Number of cities of over 500,000 inhabitants 1960	Number of cities of over 500,000 inhabitants 1975
Iraq	35	53	35	62	1	2
Kuwait	75	33	0	0	0	0
Saudi Arabia	15	17	0	22	0	2
Bahrain	n.a.	43	n.a.	0	0	0
Qatar	n.a.	85	n.a.	0	0	0
UAE	n.a.	84	n.a.	0	0	0
Oman	n.a.	6	n.a.	0	0	0
Yemen A.R.	n.a.	28	0	0	0	0
P.D.R. Yemen	61	53	0	0	0	0
Jordan	31	36	0	36	0	1
Syria	35	33	35	56	1	2
Lebanon	64	77	64	77	1	1
Egypt	38	39	53	54	2	2
Sudan	30	30	0	30	0	1
Libya	57	62	0	62	0	1
Tunisia	40	32	40	32	1	1
Algeria	27	14	27	14	1	1
Morocco	32	28	32	28	1	1
Mauritania	n.a.	n.a.	0	0	0	0
Somalia	n.a.	n.a.	0	0	0	0

Source: The World Bank, *World Development Report 1979*, Annex Table 20.

In the second place, the volume of the exodus from the countryside to urban centres is no indication of the size of excess rural population. While substantial underemployment exists in agriculture, this is only true of certain seasons of the year. Virtually all the rural labour force is engaged in the peak seasons. Mechanization has no doubt made a part of the rural labour force redundant, but not on a vast scale. Indeed, the expanded use of pesticides and fertilizers, the wider spread of extension services, the provision of adequate public and ancillary services for the villages, the intensification of agriculture, and the expansion of mixed farming, will, once they take effect, together guarantee the absorption of a substantial proportion of the underemployment in gainful employment. Furthermore, the revival of agriculture and of the rural sector in general, both economically and socially, would at least stop the drain of population, if not reverse it.

The urgency of such a revival can be seen through two indicators out of many that can be identified apart from urbanization. These are, first, the sluggishness of the agricultural sector in comparison with all the other sectors, and, secondly, the steeply growing dependence on imports of agricultural produce, and particularly of food products. The serious imbalance in the man/land relationship in the Arab region is clear in both instances.

What is meant by sluggishness is not the relative slowness of the growth of the agricultural sector over the years, compared with the other sectors, for it has been a deliberate policy of most Arab countries, since independence, to restructure their economies in such a way as to permit the faster growth of industry, construction, power generation, transport and communication, and the vital public services of education and health. We do not imply that this restructuring away from agriculture was necessarily a wise policy to pursue, but merely indicate that the system of priorities, as seen by the decision-makers in virtually all countries adopting planning and some substantial control of their economies, in effect assigned a lower place in investment priorities to agriculture than to the other sectors, particularly manufacturing industry. Rather, the sluggishness which is here deplored is that agriculture, over the past two decades for which data are available in sectoral detail, has in the vast majority of cases registered a rate of growth lower than the average rate for each economy, one which was even negative in some instances.

As a result, the relative contribution of agriculture to Gross Domestic Product (GDP) has shrunk considerably over the years.[17]

This development stands in sharp contrast to the situation in the early thirties. National accounts were not then available for any Arab country, and the whole concept of national accounting in the world and the techniques of measurement of national aggregates were both in their early phases of development. But there are many indications from individual countries to suggest that agriculture played a much more significant role in national Arab economies than it does today. This it did in four ways: in absorbing over two-thirds of the population in the countryside, in all countries except those of the Arabian Peninsula where agricultural land is very scarce; in providing employment for a portion of the active labour force considerably in excess of its counterpart today; in contributing somewhere between one-quarter and one-half of GDP; and in supplying the region as a whole with virtually all its basic needs in the way of food products. Today the position is different on each of these scores. Thus, urbanization is draining the countryside of substantial numbers of persons, including some of the most enterprising and better educated elements; agricultural employment as a ratio of total employment is dropping fast, not because of mechanization but mainly because of slackening agricultural activity; the contribution of the agricultural sector to GDP in those countries in which it used to be high today ranges between 10 and 25 per cent, or roughly half its earlier level, without this being compensated for by the expanded contribution of manufacturing industry; and the region is a net importer of food products to the tune of $6.8 billion for 1978.[18]

This last serious development is attributable only in part to the increased aggregate population, the increased consumption of foodstuffs, and the shift towards foreign-produced food products. It is mainly attributable to the slow or even negative rate of growth of agricultural production both per capita and in total, as the two sets of figures in Table 6 show. The first relates to the dozen years preceding 1950 (the earliest period for which reliable data are available), or roughly 1938–50. However, it presents the index numbers

TABLE 6

Indices of per capita production of total agriculture and food production, 1938–78

A. 1938–50: Agricultural Production (prewar = 100)

Country	Index 1949/50
Algeria	94
Egypt	115
French Morocco	96
Tunisia	120

B. 1961–78

	Index 1969–71 (1961–5 = 100)		Index 1978 (1969–71 = 100)	
Country	Total Agriculture	Food Production	Total Agriculture	Food Production
Iraq	105	104		
Saudi Arabia	108	108	110	110
Syria			137	151
Lebanon	103	102		
Egypt	103	104		
Sudan	121	120		108
Libya			161	163
Tunisia			124	124
Morocco	113	113		
Somalia	102	102		

Notes:

A. No indices are shown in the source for any other Arab country for 1938–50.

B. The indices not recorded above for the years 1961–78, and those for all the countries not listed, are all below 100: that is, they indicate a drop in per capita production.

Sources: For A., FAO, *Yearbook of Food and Agricultural Statistics, 1950*, vol. IV, Part 1, Table 123. For B., FAO, *FAO Production Yearbook, 1973* (Tables 7–10) and *FAO Production Yearbook, 1978* (Tables 4–7).

for total agricultural production for only four countries for the year 1949/50, with the prewar few years as base (= 100). The second covers almost two decades (1961–78) at the end of the half-century under consideration, both for total agricultural production and for food production. Six countries are not included in this second set of figures: Djibouti, Kuwait, United Arab Emirates, Bahrain, Qatar, and Oman, but five of these have a negligible agricultural activity anyway. The first set shows a *drop* in the index for Algeria and French

Morocco, but an increase for Egypt and Tunisia of 15 and 20 per cent respectively over a dozen years – an increase which was insufficient to cope with the population increase in Egypt, and barely sufficient in the case of Tunisia.

Without going into detail country by country for the period 1961–78, we can see that with regard to both total and per capita agricultural production, and to total and per capita food production, the general record has been poor. Only one country has registered growth in per capita production, both of general agricultural and of food products: Saudi Arabia. But even in this instance, the overall record is positive essentially because the base for comparison is very small. The second observation is that although over the sixties, five countries registered modest growth and two substantial growth in per capita production, both in general agriculture and in food products, over the seventies five of these dropped out and three appeared for the first time. (The listing in Table 6 shows only the countries with positive per capita growth rates, first in the sixties and then in the seventies.) One overall conclusion can be drawn from the two sets of figures considered together: over the forty-one years covered, 1938–78, the per capita production of agriculture and food in the countries concerned has increased very slowly and erratically. The Arab region is therefore urgently called upon to correct this situation of pressing food insufficiency, along with the undertaking of a serious and energetic drive for industrialization.

Five factors have to be brought in for a marked improvement in the performance of the agricultural sector to be possible, given the region's natural endowments in land and water, and a keen desire to promote the sector. These are: (1) the availability of adequate investible resources (for machinery, irrigation and drainage, terracing); (2) the elaboration of sound policies and plans or programmes for agricultural development; (3) the generation of enough purchasing power domestically and/or the building of markets externally to absorb the expanding production; (4) the training of manpower in the requisite skills, and (5) the implementation of agrarian reform measures wherever necessary (including the provision of technical and extension services for the rural areas). The first three factors will not engage our attention at this point. The fourth, the education and training of manpower, is so critical for the development of all sectors – and, indeed, of the whole economy and society – that it deserves separate treatment and will be undertaken in Chapter 3. The last factor, agrarian reform, will be dealt with briefly in the concluding part of the present chapter.

There is no one generally accepted definition of the content of agrarian reform. We use the term here to mean a large package of institutional, economic, and technical measures including, *inter alia*, the redistribution of land ownership in order to eliminate both excessively large land holdings and tiny, uneconomical ones; the introduction of greater rationality into the patterns of water use and crop rotation; the establishment of agricultural co-operatives; the provision of extension services; the provision of cheap agricultural credit; and the promotion of a wide mix of large-scale operation along with smaller-scale ownership. It is safe to say that nowhere in the Arab region has agrarian reform in this rather idealized and far-reaching form been implemented successfully.

Nevertheless, five countries have attempted to introduce agrarian reform together with its main components. These are Egypt, Syria, Iraq, Algeria, and Libya. Their measures of reform have spanned roughly two decades, beginning in 1952, when Egypt pioneered the institutionalization of land reform, and ending with Algeria and Libya in the early 1970s. In addition, five other countries have instituted partial measures of reform, in the sense that these measures either affected only part of the cultivable land in the country or included only some of the major components of reform. This second category of countries includes Sudan, Jordan, Tunisia, Morocco, and Saudi Arabia.

The first and obvious test of successful agrarian reform is its ability, thanks to its operation in combination with the other factors listed earlier, to effect an appreciable expansion of agricultural production. Important as this touchstone is, it has, however, to be used in conjunction with others. These include the improvement of the income and well-being of the rural population, the reduction of landlessness, the increase of the volume of employment in the countryside (basically in direct agricultural activities, but also in ancillary activities and in agro-industries), the liberation of the peasants from the grip of money-lenders and rural notables, the extension of the range of local self-government, and the improvement of the terms of tenancy and of employment for tenants and agricultural labour respectively.

We need not make a detailed examination of the record of agrarian reform, whether full reform, as in the first group of countries, or partial, as in the second group, in order to reach an overall assessment of its degree of success. Studies and observations by a number of competent authorities, and, in a few cases, official reports, together lead to the conclusion that agrarian reform has had a mixed effect, but that on balance it has fallen distinctly short of expectations. Its main failing has been in the area of increasing productivity and total production. Its main achievement, on the other hand, has been in the area of improving tenancy terms. Furthermore, the performance of agrarian reform within these two poles has varied from country to country.

The shortfall of agrarian reform can be attributed to several factors. One of these is the much slower process of redistribution of land expropriated from the owners of large landholdings, compared with the process of expropriation. A second is the imbalance between the adequacy of the legal framework governing the land expropriation and redistribution operations, and the inadequacy and slowness of the machinery implementing the relevant legislation. A third, also relating to manpower, has been the failure to train the personnel and build the institutions, quickly enough and in sufficient numbers, that were to replace the expropriated landowners and the institutions that enabled them to perform their entrepreneurial, managerial, financial, and technical functions. A fourth factor has been the frequent changes in the laws and regulations governing land reform and the irresoluteness of reform policies, which often arose from the influence of vested interests on government authorities and were aimed at aborting reform laws and regulations.

Finally, there has been insufficient motivation to guide the new beneficiaries of agrarian reform, or insufficient awareness of the true benefits of this reform, which has been manifest in such self-defeating practices as under-utilization of the newly acquired land, or its lease to other operators, and lack of enthusiasm for co-operative societies and efforts to combine individual ownerships for the purpose of more rational operation.

If there is one lesson to be learnt from the region's experience in the field of agrarian reform, it is that the preparation of the socio-psychological framework is at least as vital to success as that of the legal framework, and that the decentralization of political as well as economic decision-making is much more conducive to genuine support for reform than the issuance of directives and decisions from the central authority. Naturally, the process of popular participation takes time to promote and consolidate, as does the process of guiding the rural population in its new role and the establishment of the appropriate institutions to fill the vacuum created by the disappearance of the large landlords.

The first instance of what we earlier called 'partial agrarian reform' is the vast Gezira scheme in the Sudan, which dates as far back as 1904, but which became a remarkable operation in the three following decades. Elsewhere, in Jordan, Tunisia, Morocco, and Saudi Arabia, the so-called land reform schemes refer mainly to projects of irrigated areas for which special laws and regulations were initiated purporting to govern the settlement of farmers in these areas (as in Saudi Arabia), or to deal with land expropriated from European settlers (as in Tunisia and Morocco), or to introduce rationality into the ownership and cultivation patterns of newly irrigated localities of special significance to the country (as in the case of the Ghor Valley scheme to the east of the Jordan river in Jordan).[19] All these examples of partial reform (except in Sudan) relate to the two decades following 1956. Except for the Gezira scheme in Sudan, the impact of which has been considerable in almost every respect (production, settlement of farmers, generation of income and of foreign exchange, employment), the other examples of partial reform have generally been of marginal benefit. The Ghor Valley development programme could have become of major importance, had the Ghor not suffered from depopulation and destruction during and after the Arab–Israeli war of June 1967.

In conclusion, it can be said that if agrarian reform is to be more instrumental in the advancement of agriculture and of the whole rural sector, it must be much more effective than it has proved to be so far. To this end, it must be freed from the many and serious handicaps and shortcomings from which it has hitherto suffered. One major corrective is the education and training of manpower and its reorientation so that it may be much better equipped and motivated, and socially-directed, for the social tasks that it is called upon to handle in the process of development, both at the country level and throughout the entire Arab region. It is therefore to education and training that the discussion now turns.

3. Education and training

An assessment of the advances made in the Arab world in the area of education and technical training forms an integral part not only of the assessment of the economic development achieved but also of social and cultural development. This is because man is the instrument or driving force in each of these categories of development, and the objective or final beneficiary of all development. Consequently, very high priority is allotted to the examination of the progress made in education and training over the past half-century in the Arab world.

Casual observation might reveal spectacular, tangible achievements made in other areas, with outstanding physical evidence of change. Illustrations abound in the form of vast, highly mechanized factories, very elegant and impressive office buildings, broad modern highways, well-equipped airports, and dramatically large dams and artificial lakes. Yet progress made in the area of education is much more real and of more profound and lasting significance, in spite of all the legitimate misgivings that the observer will certainly have upon a penetrating examination of Arab education. The note of approval is based on the magnitude and directions of change with respect to education, and on the significance of such change, inasmuch as it affects the human factor which is so important for society.

It is relatively easy to record the quantitative progress made in education, expressed as absolute size of enrolment today, or as a ratio of all youth or of youth of school-age, or as manifested in the wide range of skills acquired. Further appreciation of the progress can be achieved if the progress is linked to the expansion in *each* of the three cycles of education: the elementary or primary, the secondary, and the tertiary or university levels. Quantitative assessment will be attempted straight away, although the same features in the picture cannot be reproduced for 1930 or thereabouts, owing to the dearth of comparable information. It is more difficult to make the more subtle evaluation of the quality of education, in general and on a country by country basis. Nevertheless an attempt will be made, by means of certain qualifying statements, to arrive at a balanced account of Arab education.

The most recent statistical information available shows that aggregate enrolment in all educational cycles in the Arab countries, in the public and private systems together, totalled 24.7 million in the academic year 1975/6 or 1976/7, out of an aggregate population of about 145 million at the time, or some 17 per cent of the total (see Table 7). Female enrolment constituted 35.5 per cent of total enrolment – a creditable overall proportion considering the low female enrolment in certain Arab countries and how recently female education began to be widely accepted.

The total enrolment for all three cycles lumped together tends to misrepresent the situation somewhat. This is mainly because enrolment ought to be related to youth of school age, and school attendance drops considerably (in both absolute and relative terms) as we move upwards from one cycle to the next. It would be more informative to relate enrolment in each cycle to the total number of school-age children relative to that cycle. This, however, is not feasible because information on age structure is not available for all twenty-one Arab countries and because the school age considered appropriate for each cycle varies from one country to another. The comparison between actual enrolment and school-age population has therefore been made for the first two cycles and for age-groups between 5 and 19 years lumped together. This comparison shows that 60 per cent of youth in the school-age years were actually enrolled. If we assume that females constitute roughly half the school-age youths, then female enrolment amounts to 43 per cent of school-age girls – a distinctly lower proportion than that for boys, which is 78.4 per cent.

The record of the Arab countries must be looked at in the broader context of the Third World, as well as in historical perspective within the region itself. Comparison shows that school enrolment in most Arab countries in 1975–6 was somewhat below the averages for Third World countries grouped according to income ranges. (This is the method of

TABLE 7

Arab countries: school enrolment by level of education and percentage of population aged 5–24 years (1000 students)

Country	Primary level	Secondary level	of which technical	University level	Total	Percentage of population (b) age 5–19	Percentage of female participation
Iraq	2,004.2	600.0	(28.4)	86.1	2,690.3	57.4	34.5
Kuwait	119.1	111.2	(1.9)	9.9	240.2	65.7	46.4
Saudi Arabia	701.6	222.8	(4.8)	26.4	950.8	34.5	34.1
Bahrain	48.3	18.5	(2.2)	0.7	67.5	75.1	32.3
Qatar	27.3	10.3	(0.4)	0.9	38.5	52.1	47.3
UAE	69.0	15.2	(0.6)	–	84.2	64.3	43.7
Oman	54.8	1.4	(0.1)	–	56.2	18.8	26.8
Yemen A.R.	255.6	24.2	(0.6)	2.4	282.2	16.4	11.1
P.D.R. Yemen	198.0	39.7	(0.7)	0.9	238.6	42.2	28.8
Jordan (a)	416.7	185.7	(7.5)	9.3	611.7	58.1	44.8
Syria	1,352.8	512.2	(23.7)	73.7	1,938.7	56.1	37.4
Lebanon	497.7	174.7	(3.9)	n.a.	672.4	59.0	n.a.
Egypt	4,162.9	2,107.9	(377.5)	455.1	6,725.9	43.8	36.8
Sudan	1,217.5	327.0	(9.2)	21.3	1,565.8	21.7	35.6
Libya	600.4	198.3	(5.0)	12.0	810.7	75.6	43.6
Tunisia	991.9	230.7	(69.5)	23.1	1,245.7	53.6	38.6
Algeria	2,785.3	615.3	(11.8)	52.4	3,453.0	50.1	39.2
Morocco	2,093.4	529.0	(64.1)	45.3	2,667.7	38.1	33.9
Mauritania	72.9	n.a.	n.a.	n.a.	72.9	15.8	n.a.
Somalia	230.2	12.4	(2.8)	2.0	244.6	19.6	34.6
Djibouti	9.9	2.0	(0.6)	–	11.9	25.8	32.8
Total (c)	17,909.5	5,938.5	(615.3)	821.5	24,669.5	42.4	35.5

n.a. = not available. — = none or negligible.

Notes:

(*a*) Data refer to East bank only.

(*b*) Excluding age-groups normally enrolled at university level.

(*c*) For countries where population breakdown by age is not given, it was estimated that 39 per cent of the population is in the 5–19 years intervals.

Sources: (1) *Unesco Statistical Yearbook 1978*. (2) Population data were obtained from Economic Commission for Western Asia, *1968–1977 Statistical Abstract of the Region of the Economic Commission for Western Asia*, and UN, *Statistical Yearbook 1978*.

grouping used in the World Bank's *World Development Report*.) The exceptions to this generalization are few. Another and more significant feature was that the adult literacy rates in the vast majority of Arab countries were lower in 1975 than the averages for the relevant income reference groups.[20] Thus, what has been said about the immense strides made in education in the Arab World, in terms of expansion of enrolment, applies also to other Third World regions, particularly to Latin America and non-Arab Asia.

However, it is interesting to note the absence of uniformity in the pattern, with enrolment rates being higher in certain Arab countries than the reference Third World averages for elementary education but lower for secondary education, or vice versa. The most uniform feature in the comparison is the generally lower adult literacy rate in the Arab world, and the generally slightly higher rate for enrolment in third-cycle educational institutions.

Yet the performance of the Arab world in the field of education ought to be assessed against the base level set for comparison. This level was extremely low by the First World War. More than seven centuries of steep decline separate the contemporary Arab world from its glorious cultural and scientific past, with the devastating Mogul invasions and the centuries of Ottoman domination intervening. By the turn of the twentieth century, the Arab world had lost all but a tiny fraction of its initial cultural and scientific advantage; even the Arabic language, which is held in great reverence, was mastered by relatively few. The European colonialism that followed did little to revive education, although many more schools were opened, in both the public and the private sectors, and European languages (French, English, and Italian) were added to the curricula. It is within this context that the past two or three decades of independence in the Arab world must be viewed in respect of the marked progress achieved in the field of education.

As stated earlier, this progress manifested itself strikingly in the expansion in enrolment, in both absolute and relative terms (as reflected in Table 7). It is reflected in the modernization of the curricula and methods of education, although here a great deal remains to be desired. It is also reflected in the widening of the range of academic subjects, and in the speed of the movement into the third cycle of education. By the beginning of the fifty years under survey here, there were only nine universities (or institutions of higher learning) in the Arab world: two national and one foreign in Egypt, a national one in Tunisia and another in Morocco, two private and foreign-run in Lebanon, a national one in Syria, and one in Algeria which was virtually closed to the Algerians and open only to the *colons*. Three of the nine were mainly centres of religious learning.

Today there are fifty-five universities in the region and several university centres (or university-level institutions) in addition. Four of the universities specialize mainly in theology; the rest have the regular components of sciences, arts, and humanities. With the exception of three foreign-financed and foreign-run universities (in Lebanon and Egypt), the remainder are all domestically financed, and virtually all the financing comes from government. In a couple of instances, in Lebanon and Sudan, the universities are branches of Egyptian universities and are financed mainly by the sponsoring institution.[21]

In addition to the large number of university students in the Arab region, there are tens of thousands of Arab students receiving higher education in non-Arab countries – mainly in the United States, Western Europe, and the socialist countries. (Total enrolment in university-level education exceeded one million in 1980.) But, whether at home or abroad, Arab university students are slowly but unmistakably making a shift from high concentration in literature, law, and commerce or business administration to natural sciences and the related professions (engineering, medicine) and to certain 'arts' courses more concerned with development, such as economics and education.

This is not the place for a thoroughgoing evaluation of Arab education. In any case, it is much more difficult to undertake qualitative evaluation than quantitative measurement. However, a few general remarks, based essentially on a number of government studies and appraisals of the Arab educational systems, will be sufficient for the present purpose, which is to qualify the quantitative picture and to identify the main misgivings about the region's educational performance.

The qualifications will apply in differing degrees to different countries, but they are generally applicable to the region as a whole.[22]

The first critical observation to be made is that substantial drop-outs occur between the elementary and the secondary levels of education, as Table 7 shows. Thus, roughly one-third only of pupils enrolled in elementary education stay on for secondary education, and roughly one-seventh of the latter find their way to higher education. The drop-out between the first and second cycles is the more serious phenomenon, not only because it is much more important for the pupils to move on to the secondary level of education, and thus consolidate the elementary foundation acquired, but also, and more importantly, because many of the drop-outs from the elementary cycle soon lapse back into illiteracy or near-illiteracy. This lapse constitutes a vast waste of effort, funds, and manpower.

A second criticism relates to the modesty of female enrolment, which represents today a little over one-third of total enrolment, while the female school-age population is one-half of the total. Female enrolment has, however, made remarkable progress during the independence years, considering the low base from which it started. It is worth noting that in all the six less-developed Arab countries except Sudan, the female proportion of school enrolment is extremely low. Furthermore, in certain countries, the curricula in girls' schools are not as wide-ranging or modern as in boys' schools, and the teachers are not as well trained. The narrowness of job opportunities for women outside the house and agriculture results in the wastage of much of the learning acquired in school.

The third criticism centres on technical and vocational training. Only a tiny part of secondary enrolment is actually in technical training: about 10.3 per cent of the total. (The proportion is over 40 per cent in most West European industrial countries.) Obviously, the reservoir of skilled manpower is larger than the modest ratio of 10.3 per cent suggests, including as it does those already trained, those acquiring on-the-job training, and those in elementary-level technical training institutions. However, even with all the categories of skilled manpower accounted for, there is still a serious shortage of skills compared with the urgent needs of the Arab economies.

A few indicators will help to pinpoint this shortage. Thus, even familiar occupations are becoming more demanding and their techniques more complicated. Furthermore, many new skills are becoming necessary all the time, as new industries and new technologies emerge. Finally, the sheer size of the global need is overwhelming, with development plans providing enormous investment allocations and creating vastly expanding job opportunities for skilled manpower. Thus, the development plans for the period 1975–80 for eighteen countries involved allocations totalling some $326 billion. Even assuming a modest level of plan execution, the manpower needed to undertake all the tasks involved is well beyond what is available. Indeed, the low level of execution is itself largely caused by the shortage of many skills, not only at the level of labour but also at the executive, managerial, and professional levels.[23]

The fourth and most telling criticism relates to the quality of education and of technical training. The shortcomings in this area are encountered in the content of curricula, the methodology of education and of training, the approach to and the areas of emphasis in education, the relevance of education and training to society's pressing needs and the solution of its urgent problems, the degree of creativeness and innovation in education, and its social orientation as against the orientation and motivation of the individual.

Many educators, and the more concerned citizens and decision-makers, in Arab society are anxious about the inadequacy of education and training in relation to the issues mentioned. Of special significance for a study like the present one is the complaint that education in the Arab countries has little relevance to the needs and problems of society and the economy, and is not primarily of the problem-solving type. Furthermore, it essentially prepares, or purports to prepare, individuals for their successful upgrading in their attempt to climb the economic and social ladder, and is minimally oriented to the implanting of the notions of public service in Arab youth. As far as methodology is concerned, education still fails to provide sufficient scope for innovation and intellectual stimulation, and concentrates instead on cramming the students' memories with information. Furthermore, there is insufficient practical work and experimentation in workshops, classrooms, and laboratories. These deficiencies in the educational system constitute serious hindrances to the emergence of education as a strong influence in shaping those outlooks and imparting those capabilities and attitudes most conducive to development.

Yet, telling as these types of criticism are, and modest as the quantitative achievements may be in comparison with the levels of education and training achieved in the advanced industrial countries, education in the Arab world today compares very favourably, both quantitatively and qualitatively, with that of the early 1930s. It is difficult to quantify and evalute education of fifty years ago owing to the dearth of statistics and evaluative studies. But we have enough indicators to help us see the contrast between 1930 and 1980.

Literacy rates are available only for Egypt and Palestine for the initial years of the half-century under examination. The data for the Palestinian Arabs cannot be used in a comparison with the situation of the Palestinians today, under the diaspora, although there are many indicators to suggest a considerable rise in the rate of literacy from 15.9 per cent of Palestinian Arabs in 1931 (or of 11.6 per cent for persons over 14 years of age). Informed guesses put the level at par with the highest in the Arab world, or somewhere around 65 per cent for the whole population. Comparable data exist only for Egypt, but here again the data for 1927 and 1937 (two census years around our initial year, which is 1930) relate to the whole population. The literacy rates were 13.7 per cent and 18.6 per cent for the two census years respectively. By 1975, the ratio for adults had risen to 44 per cent.[24]

Egypt, Palestine, and Lebanon, but particularly the last, were ahead of the other Arab countries in educational efforts at the start of the half-century under examination. But even here enrolment absorbed a much smaller proportion of children of school age than it does today. Thus, in the early 1930s in Egypt, where efforts to speed education dated as far back as the beginnings of Mohammed Ali's reign early in the nineteenth century, 942,000 pupils were enrolled in public elementary schools, and 15,000 (including only 1,500 girls) in secondary schools. The private school system was more active than the public system at the secondary level of education, accounting for five to six times as many students as the public system. The proportion of girls in private schools (mainly European mission schools) was much higher than in the public system, reaching a little over two-fifths.[25] In all, there were just over a million youths enrolled in schools in Egypt between 1933 and 1935: only 7 per cent of the total population then, or one-fifth of children of school age. Today the latter proportion is about three-fifths.

A few indicators relating to other countries provide us with a clearer picture of the rudimentary state of education in the early 1930s. Thus, in North Sudan (which was and remains more advanced than South Sudan) total school enrolment in 1930 numbered 41,296, in which female enrolment accounted for 1,966 or 4.8 per cent. Low as enrolment was then, it gave no indication of the size of modern education, for 28,669 of the youths enrolled (over 69 per cent) were in *katateeb*[26] – Quranic schools attached to mosques where only rudimentary reading and arithmetic were taught, in addition to the memorizing of the Holy Qur'an. The population of North Sudan in 1930 was estimated at 5.5 million[27] – which shows how marginal school enrolment was at the time.

Libya, a much smaller country than Sudan, with a population of 715,000 in 1931, had 6,754 pupils in elementary schools for Arabs. (The first secondary school was reported in 1935.) But Algeria presents a gloomier picture. As late as 1944, 90 per cent of students in all schools were European, while the European community constituted only 10 per cent of total population. (The Jewish community was usually listed as 'European', because it was non-Muslim.) The illiteracy rate among Muslims was as high as 94 per cent of the population.[28] It should be recalled that by 1944 the French had been in control of Algeria for 114 years, a period long enough surely for a European country with a *mission civilisatrice* to produce some creditable educational results!

If we turn to the Asian Arab countries, we find that

Transjordan, with an estimated population in 1931 of 300,000, had a total of 4,698 pupils in public schools, and only a few hundred more in private schools. In the same year, Iraq, whose population numbered 3.3 million, had a total enrolment in the public system of 36,834, which included 34,513 in the elementary cycle, 2,082 in the secondary cycle, 140 in vocational schools, and 99 in higher education abroad.[29] As in the case of Transjordan, private education accounted for a small number in addition to the enrolment cited.

The situation was distinctly better on the littoral of the Mediterranean. Thus, Syria, with a population of 2 million, had in 1932 a total enrolment of 103, 531 pupils (in addition to 26,000 in Quranic schools). Just over half of these, or 52.5 per cent, were in public schools, the rest being in private schools, both domestic and foreign. The position of private education was even stronger in Lebanon, where, again in 1932, with a total population of just over 862,000, there was a total enrolment of 104,133, of whom the private sector accounted for 84.9 per cent or 88,427 students. (The foreign schools alone accounted for just over one-third of total enrolment.) It should be added that this total included all three cycles of education, with 1,929 in the two (foreign) universities in Beirut, and 205 trainees in technical schools. On the other hand, the total for Syria included only 496 students in higher education, but 2,197 in technical training.[30] It is obvious that Lebanon was far ahead of all other Arab countries in terms of enrolment at all levels of education, in relation to its population. The other special feature, as indicated elsewhere in this section, was the pre-eminence of the private sector, which accounted for all secondary and higher education.

Progress over the period is worth mentioning with respect to six other countries. Lebanon occupies the seat of honour as a country with high levels of literacy, education, and technical training today, and – as already observed – an early start in this respect. It stands out as the country with the largest role for private education. As late as the early seventies, private education had a larger enrolment than public education at the first and second levels combined. Even today enrolment in private secondary schools is larger than in public schools, and female enrolment is very high, particularly in the former.

The other countries to which special reference is made here are Iraq, Jordan, Syria, Kuwait, and Algeria. All five show a creditable record in educational performance, but the first three had an earlier start than the last two. Kuwait can boast the highest rate of literacy in the Arab world today along with Iraq, as well as a very high ratio of enrolment. Iraq's record also reveals serious efforts in the field of education and training, and the financial means to support this effort. On the other hand, Jordan, whose progress is more recent than Iraq's though earlier than Kuwait's, has not the material resources of either but is as strongly determined as they are. Syria was an early starter in energetic educational effort, as mentioned earlier in this chapter.

Finally, Algeria deserves special mention, although it still has to struggle against a high rate of adult illiteracy (some 65 per cent in 1975). Algeria had to fight against heavy odds when it finally got its independence in 1962. The whole educational system, from elementary to university level, had been geared primarily to serve the French and the non-Muslim inhabitants. In fact, the University of Algiers began admitting Algerians only shortly before independence, and then on a selective basis, selection being tied to the political affinity of the parents with the colonialists. On the eve of independence, there were only two Algerian engineers in the country.[31] At the other extreme, the elementary schools were grossly inadequate for the country's needs, and they provided only a passable knowledge of the four R's. The national language itself was being relentlessly suppressed in order to make the population forget it. If this policy did not succeed as far as the spoken language is concerned, it succeeded with regard to classical Arabic. The secondary school system was minimal in size, restricted to the cities, and, on the whole, to the children of the French. The bourgeoisie was barely allowed to send its children to secondary schools. The Jewish community depended mainly on its own school system.

It was against such odds and a very harsh and unaccommodating background that Free Algeria had to struggle in the area of education. That it has today one of the highest ratios of enrolment in the Arab region is certainly a credit to the country's determination and the efforts and resources it is diverting to education. Furthermore, Algeria is laying special emphasis on technical training, along with Egypt, Iraq, Lebanon, Tunisia, and Morocco.

An attempt has been made to produce a balanced account of the region's performance in the fields of education and technical and vocational training. Thus, the progress made in quantitative terms has been qualified with observations relating both to its size and to its quality. These qualifications, it ought to be added, apply to the Third World countries in general, not solely to the Arab countries. Three final conclusions can be drawn with regard to the future. First, the spread of education should be accelerated, in order not only to enrol a larger proportion of school-age children, particularly of girls, and to reduce drastically the volume of drop-out between the elementary and the secondary levels but also to bring about a drastic reduction in the present high proportion of illiteracy.

The second conclusion is that the quality of education ought to be improved. Far more attention should be directed to the fundamental and urgent requirements of the society and the economy and a much more serious search should be launched for a system of education capable of preparing the young to cope with these requirements. In the course of this search considerably more attention should be paid to finding the answers to problems which emanate from society's heritage and situation, instead of the automatic, uncritical copying of external formulas that we witness today.

Thirdly, the young should be given much more encouragement to seek and obtain technical training, instead of drifting, as at present, in large numbers towards general secondary education which, at best, can prepare them only for clerical jobs. Among other things, the shift in the pattern of education involves concern with the values governing the behaviour of the young in this respect, and an attempt to inculcate those values appropriate to the shift.

A final point must be emphasized. It is that the Arab countries' achievements in the field of education have almost all been identified with the era of independence. It is, then, up to the free national will of the Arabs to consolidate and advance these educational achievements and to regain a place of eminence in the fields of science and culture worthy of the Arab past.

4. Arab oil and gas: precarious pre-eminence

The only economic sector which started operating and contributing to the Gross Domestic Product at the beginning of the half-century which is at the centre of our study is that of oil and gas, or the hydrocarbon sector. To be precise, oil had already been found in Iraq in commercial quantities in 1927, ahead of all other Arab countries. But the quantities exported then were very small – some 40,000 tons – and the revenue received by the Iraqi government from the concessionary company was minimal. The royalty had been fixed by agreement at 4 gold shillings per ton, and the total revenue that flowed into the treasury was 7,800 pounds sterling.[32]

The forties also were a period of slow growth, whether for Iraq alone or for the first three countries to export oil, namely Iraq followed by Kuwait and Saudi Arabia. Thus Iraq 'first received annual dues in excess of one million sterling during the forties, reaching 3.2 mn in 1949. During that same year, expenditure under the national budget was 30 mn, against a total revenue of 28.6 mn.' The three countries listed 'together only received a total of about $20 mn in 1946, the first postwar year'.[33] In contrast, the total production for 1979 of the three countries combined was 16.3 million barrels per day (b/d), while it amounted to about 23m. b/d (some 1,150m. tons a year) valued at about $160 billion, for the twelve Arab oil-producing countries, both members of the Organization of Petroleum Exporting Countries and non-members.[34] In effect, therefore, the emergence and fast growth of the hydrocarbon sector, and its arrival at a position of pre-eminence, all occurred within the period under examination, 1930–80.

The significance of oil and gas* is not limited to such

*In the course of the discussion the word 'oil' will be used to mean hydrocarbons in general unless the context requires specific reference to gas, or to oil and gas together.

aggregates as volume of production or export, or total revenues. Oil is a resource of great, indeed, strategic, significance which is crucial for industry, transport, household use, and military capability. This characterization applies to energy in general, but in its specifics it applies only to oil and gas. This is because other forms of energy can serve one or more of the uses just enumerated, mainly as fuel or a source of power. But it is oil and gas only that combine in themselves the functions of fuel as well as feedstock for industry. In the latter instance, hydrocarbon-based industries (petrochemical industries) produce hundreds of different products that range from fertilizers to proteins, and include a very wide variety of synthetics, dyes, plastic products, and fabrics. Yet even as a fuel, both oil and gas have distinct advantages over other forms of energy such as coal and nuclear power.

By the end of 1979 the Arab oil-producing countries accounted for 34 per cent of total oil production in the world. Their proven reserves then were 334,840 million barrels. This volume would permit production for another forty years at the 1979 average of production, assuming there is no change in the estimate of proven reserves.[35]

The finiteness of this most valuable resource calls for an urgent pause for thought. Three significant conclusions emerge even from the briefest consideration of the issue. First, that the revenues derived from the export of oil should not, strictly speaking, be considered a component of GDP or of national income, since they do not arise from an economic activity which is income-generating on a continuous, self-renewing basis: indeed, what occurs is the exchange of one asset (oil) for another (financial resources) through the process of sale or exporting. The second conclusion flows from the first. It is that, as soon as possible, the Arab oil-exporting countries must transform their oil resources into productive capability: in other words, use their oil revenues as speedily and judiciously as possible as an engine of economic and social development. And thirdly, that the owners of the hydrocarbon resource should control it and take all the decisions relating to it. There will be occasion to discuss certain aspects of these three points at greater length in the last chapter of the book. They are mentioned here in passing because of their relevance and immediacy for the discussion of the Arab oil and gas sector, and its development over the past half-century.

Until the early seventies, this development was almost entirely in the hands of the concessionary companies which handled all matters relating to the resource, from exploration and drilling to production, pricing, and export. In addition, they undertook refining and transport by pipelines and tankers. While most of the accompanying gas was flared and thus wasted, a very small proportion was used, beginning in the sixties, as fuel (mainly for the desalination of water and the generation of electricity, but also for industry) by some of the producing countries. It is only since 1973 that petrochemical industries have begun to be established in the region, thus providing the scope for a more substantial use of gas. All significant decisions relating to the oil industry, in all its ramifications, were taken by the oil companies up to the early seventies.

National sovereignty over resources is a natural and inalienable right of states, and to this extent the Arab governments always had the legal right to own and exercise control over the oil sector. But in practice, they relinquished this right by signing concession agreements with major foreign oil commpanies. This was done in effect under duress, in so far as most of the concessions were given, while European colonial powers exercised political control over the countries concerned, to transnational companies belonging to the Western countries. An additional factor was the underdevelopment of the Arab oil countries and their inability to run all aspects of the oil industry themselves. These two factors together resulted first in the oil countries obtaining very unfavourable terms from the concessionary companies, and secondly in the failure of these companies to train Arab nationals in the managerial and technical skills required to enable them to take over effective, substantive decision-making.

It was only in October 1973 that the take-over of control and decision-making was virtually completed by the oil governments. The process was dramatically crowned by a unilateral decision by the Arabian Gulf members of OPEC to adjust the oil prices upwards, in order to correct the price structure that had been kept artificially low by the oil companies throughout the period of their control. Persistent efforts, beginning in the fifties, to effect such adjustment had produced only marginal improvement for the producing countries. The process of adjustment began with the introduction of a profit-sharing formula in the early fifties, pioneered by Iraq and Saudi Arabia, but this formula had little practical effect, inasmuch as the posted price of oil remained very low. Even the strong attempts made later on, and accelerated in the late sixties and early seventies, failed to bring about a substantial increase in the revenue per unit of export received by government. Thus, the governments acquiesced in the production of an increased volume of oil – and therefore the unduly fast depletion of this most valuable non-renewable resource – in order to assure themselves of adequate revenue to finance the expanding development programmes which they had been undertaking in the fifties and sixties.

The 16th of October 1973 is a historical landmark not only in so far as the correction of the price of oil is concerned but also with respect to other important areas of decision. It was a clear dividing-line between the period during which the exercise of power was abdicated and the new period when this power was recaptured by the governments, in all matters relating to the oil industry. Thus, we witness the entry of the producing countries into all aspects of the industry, both upstream and downstream. Apart from the initiation in the autumn/winter of 1973/4 of a series of grossly overdue corrective price adjustments, which have continued to be put into effect up to the start of the eighties, and apart from the complete nationalization of the assets of the oil sector in almost all Arab producing countries, a number of other areas of decision have been taken over. They include the determination of the volume of production, the determination of the destination of exports, the expansion of refining capacity, the building of tanker fleets, and the introduction of petrochemical industry. In addition, the expanded volume of revenues accruing from oil exports now permits the undertaking of very large development programmes in the oil-producing countries and, to a lesser extent, in non-oil countries.

Progress along these various lines is not, however, uniform. The determination of prices and of volume of production, and of the destination of exports, is now undertaken entirely by the national governments. But progress elsewhere is more limited, and it will be some time before a tangible achievement can be recorded. A few illustrations will suffice to prove the point: the wasteful flaring of gas has dropped noticeably for the major Arab producers as a group, from 74 to 52 per cent of gas produced for 1973 and 1978 respectively, but the drop varies in steepness between one producer and another, though it still remains high in the aggregate; refining capacity has risen by more than one-third during the seventies to reach 3.37m. b/d,[36] but it still accounts for just under 15 per cent of production for the whole Arab region (13 per cent for the twelve oil-producing countries alone). Even if account is taken of capacity being installed and expected to be in operation in 1985, it would stand at only 4.87m. b/d or 44 per cent above capacity at the beginning of 1980.[37] The Arab tanker fleet had a total capacity of 11.5m. tons d.w., or a mere 3.5 per cent of the world capacity of 330.1m. by the end of 1979.[38]

Taken together, Arab refining and transport facilities account for a small percentage of Arab production and exports respectively, although the position of Arab producers as a group in world production and in the hydrocarbon trade is much larger. (With respect to Arab oil exports, it should be stated that total Arab consumption was 1.18m. b/d in 1978, or 6 per cent of total production for that year. The balance goes into export).[39] Finally, although a great deal of investment, running into many tens of billions of dollars is planned and/or already being made in the petrochemical industry, actual production is still in its infancy, covering fertilizers and some first-phase products only. Furthermore, there is hardly any regional co-ordination in the planning and undertaking of investment in the hydrocarbon-based industry with a view to the optimization of investment. (See Tables 8–12 at the end of the chapter.)

This account ignores the effectiveness of the drive for development, which has been intensified thanks to the revenues from oil. However, the examination of the record of development will be undertaken in some detail in Chapter 9, and it would be appropriate to leave any further reference to the pattern and quality of development achieved until then. The examination of the issues deriving from and relating to the accrual of substantial oil revenue, and the accumulation of considerable financial reserves abroad for some oil exporters, will be deferred to the last chapter of the book, as one crucial issue of development. In anticipation of the forthcoming discussion, it ought, however, to be stated here that the pre-eminence which the hydrocarbon sector has acquired, and the promotive role it has played in the region's economy, must be qualified in three significant ways. The first is the fact that the hydrocarbon resource is finite and is being depleted fast, before alternative sources of energy have been developed to replace hydrocarbons, not only at competitive prices but also with comparable technical advantages.

The second qualification is the urgent need for economic and technological development that will enable the Arab economies to generate sufficient income in the years to come to make up for the inevitable drop in oil revenue, as depletion eats more and more deeply into reserves. Hence, the problem in this context goes beyond the speed with which roads, barrages, factories, and schools are being built, to extend into the profound question of the content and quality of development which is being sought and achieved with oil revenues as its engine. The third and final qualification relates closely to the preceding one. It is the 'social cost' of oil revenues or, more specifically, the effect on Arab society, work habits, consumption patterns, and values, of the inflow of a substantial revenue in the form of economic rent, and how the Arab region will minimize these social costs.

In fairness, it ought at the same time to be underlined that oil has had a positive and far-reaching effect, primarily on the exporting countries, but also on the non-exporting countries. More will be said about this aspect later, but passing reference at least should be made to the financial flows it has made possible for those Arab countries in stringent financial conditions, the manpower flows to the oil countries from other Arab countries that it has brought about to what the

TABLE 8

Crude oil production in the Arab countries in 1979 (1000 barrels/day)

Country	Production
Iraq	3,500
Kuwait	2,600
Bahrain	50
Qatar	500
UAE	1,776
Oman	295
Saudi Arabia	10,200
Syria	170
Egypt	550
Libya	2,020
Tunisia	108
Algeria	1,210
Total, Arab	22,979
Total, World	64,324

Source: *Petroleum Economist*, January 1980.

TABLE 9

Proven oil reserves in the Arab countries, end 1979 (million barrels)

Country	Reserves
Iraq	31,000
Kuwait	65,400
Bahrain	240
Qatar	3,760
UAE	29,400
Oman	2,400
Saudi Arabia	163,350
Syria	2,000
Egypt	3,100
Libya	23,500
Tunisia	2,250
Algeria	8,440
Total, Arab	334,840
Total, World	641,600

Source: *Oil and Gas Journal*, December 1979.

exchange signifies in closer Arab interaction, and to the overall impact it has had on the financing of development programmes and projects. Nevertheless, on balance, the hydrocarbon sector can still be said to have acquired a *precarious* pre-eminence which calls for concern, thought, and preventive/corrective action.

TABLE 10

OAPEC Countries: natural gas production 1978 and gas reserves, end 1979

Country	Production (million cubic metres)	Per cent flared	Reserves (trillion cubic feet)
Iraq	11,000	85.0	27.5
Kuwait	11,124	39.0	33.5
Bahrain	3,715	0.0	9.0
Qatar	4,650	68.0	60.0
UAE	13,553	63.0	20.5
Saudi Arabia	43,784	75.0	95.7
Syria (*a*)	470	0.0	1.5
Egypt	(*b*)	(*b*)	3.0
Libya	21,244	25.0	24.0
Algeria	32,517	38.0	132.0
Total, Arab	146, 294 (*c*)	52.0	406.7
Total, World	1,596,873	(*b*)	2,573.2

Notes:
(*a*) Estimate.
(*b*) Not available.
(*c*) Country data do not add up to total in the source.

Source: League of Arab States, Directorate-General of Economic Affairs, 'Oil and Gas in the Arab Homeland' (July 1980; in Arabic), Table 4, for production. *Oil and Gas Journal* for reserves.

TABLE 11

Oil consumption in the Arab countries, 1978
(1000 barrels/day)

Country	Consumption
Iraq	175.8
Kuwait	36.8
Bahrain	5.6
Qatar	8.4
UAE	10.9
Oman	23.0
Saudi Arabia	225.5
Jordan	28.6
Syria	86.0
Lebanon	42.9
Yemen A.R.	5.3
P.D.R. Yemen	12.9
Egypt	187.7
Sudan	38.7
Libya	80.2
Tunisia	38.1
Algeria	102.1
Morocco	61.4
Mauritania	3.7
Somalia	4.6
Djibouti	1.2
Total	1,179.4

Source: League of Arab States, op. cit., Table 7.

TABLE 12

Refining capacity in Arab countries
(1000 barrels/day)

Country	Existing capacity, 1979	Estimated capacity, 1985	Estimated capacity 1990
Iraq	296	320	470
Kuwait	644	644	644
Bahrain	250	250	250
Qatar	10	10	60
UAE	14	135	185
Saudi Arabia	1,005	1,625	1,875
P.D.R. Yemen	175	169	169
Jordan	25	75	75
Syria	237	237	317
Lebanon	30	30	30
Egypt	285	410	410
Sudan	26	51	51
Libya	138	138	348
Tunisia	25	85	85
Algeria	125	502	502
Morocco	78	148	298
Mauritania	–	20	20
Somalia	10	10	20
Total	3,373	4,859	5,809

Note:

Total estimated capacity, 1985 and 1990, varies very slightly from that in source (4,859 and 5,809 versus 4,867 and 5,827 respectively).

Source: League of Arab States, op. cit., Table 13.

5. Industrial first steps

The survey and assessment of manufacturing industry as it stood in the Arab region in 1930 does not lead to notable results. Not only was the industrial sector* then very tiny in size and contribution but also many of the manufacturing establishments were owned and operated by foreign nationals and companies which came mainly from the colonial powers in political control, but also from some other Western powers with no political status in the region. Several of the establishments were organized in the form of concessionary companies over which the local governments had very little or no control, and from which they levied minimal taxes or fees. Furthermore, the industries in existence in the early thirties were at a primitive technological level, that is, they involved industrial processes and products which were very elementary by the standard of the colonial countries. Finally, although there were no national accounts relating to the early thirties, there are enough indications to hand now to suggest that the industrial sector made a very tiny contribution to domestic product compared with that of agriculture and services.

The insignificance of the contribution in relative terms can be verified once it is realized that in 1980, after fifty years of change and a strong post-war drive for industrialization, the contribution is still only 7.6 per cent of GDP for the Arab region as a whole, but 16.3 per cent if oil revenues are excluded from GDP. (Manufacturing industry in the tables of the World Bank's *World Development Report* excludes water, electricity, and gas. However, these are included in the percentages shown here. But if they were excluded the proportions would drop to 6.8 and 14.6 per cent respectively.) The fact that the aggregate domestic product of the region has grown considerably in real terms in the intervening half-

*Throughout this chapter references to industry or to the industrial sector relate only to manufacturing industry.

century, and that the contribution of manufacturing industry has also registered growth, does not contradict but reinforces the statement that the relative contribution of the industrial sector must have been extremely small in 1930, since after fifty years of growth it still remains modest.

This is the picture, then, drawn in very broad strokes. However, some differentiation is called for, both with respect to countries and to types of manufacturing industry developed, if a clearer and more precise picture is to emerge of the sector at the start of the half-century under examination. Furthermore, flexibility must be allowed with respect to the starting-point of the account, inasmuch as the situation began to change noticeably during the thirties from what it had been in 1930. This is because 1929/30 was of international significance as the year of the Crash in the United States and Western Europe, which was to be followed by protracted and intensified Depression. Yet it was precisely during the thirties that a number of Arab countries were able to apply moderate protective measures and to make some increased investment in industry, as the economic grip of the colonial powers weakened and they became preoccupied with their own problems at home. In brief, while the year 1930 on its own was characterized by very little manufacturing activity in the national sector (that is, the sector in which national investors dominated and ran industry), the thirties as a whole witnessed increased investment by the national bourgeoisie.

Yet this contrast between 1930 as a single year and the decade of the thirties as a whole must not be carried too far. There were factors moving in the opposite direction which tended to dampen expectations and to restrict resources. They included the drop in purchases by the colonial powers of the raw materials that they normally imported from the region, owing to the Depression. Furthermore, investment and budgetary support in the region by the colonial powers were likewise compressed for the same reason. On balance, therefore, it was a sign of improved internal expectations that Arab investors started some new industries, even if modest in size and limited in variety, in a climate of Depression in the industrial world.

The Mashreq was more advanced than the Maghreb* with regard to *national* manufacturing industry.[40] The bulk of industry in the Maghreb had been established by and was owned and run by the *colons*, Italians in Libya, and Frenchmen in the rest of the Maghreb.[41] As to the Sudan, not much industry existed in 1930, but what did exist was owned predominantly by British firms and other non-Sudanese minority groups. The researcher therefore has to turn to the Mashreq for signs of industrial development by nationals of the countries concerned.

Egypt was the leader in such development in the Mashreq. In fact manufacturing industry there dated as far back as the early decades of the nineteenth century, during Mohammed Ali's drive for modernization. But it was Bank Misr which distinguished itself in the establishment of manufacturing industry in several fields in the twenties and thirties of the current century. The example of Bank Misr prompted other investors to set up industrial establishments. Furthermore, the removal in the mid-thirties of certain economic restrictions that had earlier been imposed on Egypt (as part of the Ottoman Empire) by the colonial powers, under what was known as the 'capitulations' system, permitted Egypt to apply some protective measures and acted as a further incentive to industry.

It is not easy to differentiate between handicrafts and manufacturing industry proper in the meagre statistics available for the thirties, but the leading industries in Egypt seem primarily to have related to, and centred on, cotton, but also sugar and rice. The most notable branches of industry were spinning and clothing, sugar refining and rice cleaning among several food industries, and cigarettes and matches; they also included metal articles, cement and other building materials, glass, modern carpet weaving, dye-making, paper articles (including printing), some simple machines and machine tools, leather, and generation of electric power. The total labour force in industry in 1927 (according to census data for that year) was a little over 492,000 of which about

*As indicated earlier, the Mashreq includes Egypt and the Asian Arab countries, while the term 'Maghreb' refers to the group of African countries composed of Libya, Tunisia, Algeria, and Morocco.

10 per cent were women. But employment in the major branches of industry alone was a little under 100,000. A word of warning is called for here: many of the manufacturing establishments consisted in effect of small workshops, barely mechanized, as the definition of 'industry' was then very elastic; the number of workers in most establishments was very small, with only a few exceptions. Furthermore, the industrial processes were not very advanced. This, plus the fact that the line between handicrafts and industry was not very clear, accounts for the large number of industrial workers reported.

Other countries in the Mashreq in which industry can be said to have made some advances in the thirties are Lebanon, Syria, and, to a lesser extent, Iraq and Palestine. Lebanon and Syria had a larger variety of industrial products than anywhere else in the Asian Arab region. These included food products and beverages, textiles, tanning and leather goods, cement, cigarettes and tobacco, matches, soap, asphalt, and electricity generation. Employment in modern establishments is reported at just over 33,000 in the main cities of the two countries, with Beirut alone accounting for over half this number, and Aleppo and Damascus together for a third.

Very much the same types of industry existed in Iraq, but the range was narrower and the level of performance lower. The main branches were food products and beverages, tanning and leather goods, soap, bricks and tiles, milling, cotton ginning and textiles, printing, and cigarettes and matches. The entire labour force for mechanized establishments numbered only a few thousand.

Manufacturing industry in Palestine in the thirties can be examined for the Arab community on its own, thanks to a few studies and official reports,[42] which present their findings in aggregates for the country as well as for the Arab and Jewish communities separately.* Arab industry was not very dissimilar from its counterpart in Syria and Lebanon. It too comprised such branches as soap, cigarettes, foodstuffs and

*Official publications followed the practice of dividing the communities on the basis of religion. We, however, group all non-Jews into one category labelled 'Arab', since non-Arab Muslims and non-Arab Christians were a negligible component numerically and economically.

beverages, milling, and olive pressing, but on the whole had a narrower range of industrial products.

Manufacturing industry in Palestine was spurred by the example of Jewish industry, which had recourse to more abundant funds and skills, but at the same time was inhibited by it because of the advantages it enjoyed and the self-containment of the Jewish community, which virtually closed its market to Arab production. Again, like its counterpart in Syria and Lebanon, Palestinian industry overlapped with handicrafts; most of the establishments had little capital and a small labour force; and it was difficult to draw the line between workshops and factories. According to information available, industry and handicrafts together engaged 22,000 workers/craftsmen in 1936, or 8 per cent of the total work-force in all sectors; production per worker was 90 Palestine pounds (equal to sterling pounds), which meant that the sector's production totalled some 2 million pounds. By the end of the thirties, according to the industrial census for 1939, there were 4,117 Arab workers engaged in manufacturing (apart from handicrafts). Gross production per worker had risen to 375 pounds, as against 442 pounds per Jewish worker. This is a telling comparison, considering the much higher level of education and training of the Jewish work-force, and the greater capital intensity of Jewish industry.[43]

By the end of the half-century under survey, Arab industry had made vast advances in the size of its work-force, both in absolute terms and as a proportion of the labour force actively engaged; in the magnitude of its value added in GDP; in the spread in the range of industries introduced; and in its technical sophistication compared with its modest beginnings. Today the industrial labour force numbers about 4 million workers, including a moderately-sized contingent of highly skilled technicians and professionals. The value added of manufacturing industry aggregated for 1979 was $22.9 billion (or $20.6 billion if electricity, water, and gas were excluded).[44] The branches of manufacturing industry introduced into the region are today considerably wider in range than those in existence half a century ago, and much more advanced in the technology applied. Furthermore, manufacturing industry is serviced by more efficient forms of organization and more advanced research and cost accounting.

With respect to the industries introduced, it can be said that although engineering industries, electronics, automotive industries, and generally sophisticated industries are as yet only nebulous, a wide range of other branches can be found in several of the countries under examination. These include car, tractor, radio, and television assembly plants; metal works; factories for electric and construction goods; medicines, dyes and paints; furniture, glass, and kitchen utensils; petroleum refining and petrochemicals; and many other products whose entry into the region is recent. Moreover, branches of manufacturing that have been in existence for decades have witnessed drastic change in their machines and tools, as well as in the quality of their products and their factory organization. Finally, there are today large industrial conglomerations, whether in branches long established in the region like textiles, foodstuffs, and cement, or in new branches such as metal-working, assembly plants, and petrochemicals.

To complete this brief characterization of the manufacturing sector as it has evolved over the past fifty years, we shall refer to the differentiation between the various countries of the region in their achievement. The first observation to be made is that the range between the more and the less advanced countries is now much wider than it was half a century ago, owing to the fact that the countries in which manufacturing industry contributed most to GDP had then a much lower relative contribution in absolute terms.

Finally, while the countries that were more advanced in 1930 in terms of industrial development continue to be advanced today, other countries have registered marked progress in industrialization in the intervening years, from very modest beginnings. Specifically, Egypt, Lebanon, and Syria continue to have a relatively active manufacturing sector (contributing about 16, 16, and 11 per cent of GDP respectively). But in addition, in four other countries the contribution is also larger than the average for the region (which is 7.6 per cent); it is 20, 12, 14, and 15 per cent in Morocco, Algeria, Tunisia, and Jordan, respectively. It is below average in each of the other countries. (In all cases, the proportion indicated relates to a broad definition of manufacturing, including electricity, gas, and water.)

The comparison of the various aspects of the sector of manufacturing industry for the two end dates, 1930 and 1980, reveals notable advances, as already indicated. However, this outcome needs to be heavily qualified in four major respects, the first of which is industrial labour. Thus, although the labour force currently engaged in manufacturing numbers some 4 million workers, as against a little over half a million in 1930, it represents only about 10 per cent of the aggregate active labour force in 1980. In other words, manufacturing industry has not met the rosy expectations of the Arab countries, when they declared themselves determined to promote energetic industrialization measures in the post-war era, with the marked expansion of employment as one of their major aims.

The second qualification relates to the value added. While the aggregate value added in the sector has grown considerably in absolute terms, to about $23 billion, which represents a vast improvement over its counterpart in 1930 even if inflationary pressures are taken into account, yet this value added is still modest in relative terms, as already stated. The clearest indication of the sluggishness of Arab industrialization can be obtained by comparison with other regions in the world, with the countries grouped according to GNP per capita as in the World Bank's *World Development Report, 1980*. In every single instance except Egypt, the contribution of manufacturing in the Arab countries is below the weighted average for the relevant income group. (In Egypt's case it is equal to the group average according to the World Bank, but much below that according to the country tables of the Arab Fund for Economic and Social Development. There is strong reason to believe that the World Bank overestimates the sector's contribution.)

In the third place, the drive for industrialization has not been accompanied by a soundly conceived and effective drive to acquire technological capability. Appropriate technology is necessary for all sectors and activities, but particularly for manufacturing industry. Grossly inadequate concern has, however, been expressed by Arab society for the need to acquire and develop the necessary scientific and technological capabilities and skills that, in the final analysis, permit a genuine, independent industrial capability, and without which such a capability is impossible.

In more recent years, the region has been gripped by a desire for the 'transfer of technology', but this transfer has come to be understood as the purchase of modern capital goods (machines, tools, equipment), and the 'purchase' of the services of foreign technicians and experts. Nothing could be further from a genuine transfer of technology than such a course. In fact, this course makes the transfer harder to effect. What looks like a longer course of action, namely, the development of science, research, experimentation, and technical training, is in effect the *true* short-cut to technological capability. Furthermore, although such development may seem costly, in fact its cost represents fruitful investment. On the other hand, continued excessive dependence on the importation of foreign machines and skills is a much costlier course, and one which does not promise independence. As far as cost, is concerned, it has been estimated that the Arab region has been paying about $5 billion a year over the past few years for the purchase of technological software, namely, skills, patents, managerial and training assistance, and design and consultancy services. In addition, billions of dollars leak outside the region for the purchase of certain simple machines, tools, and equipment that could be produced by Arab industry right away or with minor preparation.[45]

Finally, the fourth qualification necessary for a correct assessment of Arab manufacturing industry today is that the range of industries established and products turned out is still narrow, and the quality of products leaves a great deal to be desired, if industry is to achieve the dual success of providing substitutes for imports on a large scale and of competing in export markets. In both instances success is very limited. Although the performance of manufacturing industry differs widely between one country and another, even where it is at its highest level, it still falls far short of the two criteria just mentioned.

The relatively modest progress achieved by the sector of

manufacturing industry during the fifty years under examination, particularly in the post-war period 1945–80, needs explaining. This is because of the emphasis placed on industrialization in developmental plans and projects, the resources directed to that purpose, and the belief in the value of industry as the central mechanism in the strategy of development, and the means for and touchstone of economic independence parallel with political independence. If the explanation is to be summed up in one statement, it would be that the drive for industrialization has suffered from the haziness of the concept of the nature and role of industry among decision-makers in most Arab countries, as well as from the inadequate understanding of the notion of sectoral balance in the economy, and finally from confusion and frequent change in the social and economic institutional frameworks within which industrialization has proceeded.

The need for explanation justifies some further elaboration of this condensed generalization.[46] A review of industrial policies shows, first, that the aims sought varied between import-substitution, export, self-sufficiency, and the transfer of technology via industrial development. (Obviously, the identity and quality of goods produced is a very important by-product of the choice of aims.) But beyond this, there has been insufficient appreciation of what industrial capability in fact signifies, by way of control over the use and transformation of resources, industrial discipline, industrial rationality, and labour and corporate organization congruous with industrialization.[47] As in the case of the confusion between the mere importation of modern machines and the resort to the technical skills of foreigners, on the one hand, and the true transfer of technology (or, more appropriately, the acquisition of technological capability), on the other, there has been a confusion between the building of modern factories capable of producing a widening array of consumer goods and some intermediate and capital goods, and industrialization in a true, much more far-reaching sense.

A second explanation for the modest progress in industrial development has been the indecision relating to the various social systems or system combinations thought most conducive to industrial development, and frequent changes in this policy area. We refer here to the ideological and practical conflicts between the pre-eminence of the public sector, the private sector, or the mixed sector; between 'socialism' and 'free enterprise'; between the degree of centralization and free choice to be adopted; and the seriousness, reach, and efficiency of planning versus the 'free market' mechanism, or even versus a combination of the two. Not only has there been conflict (frequently ideological/intellectual, always informational, and sometimes political) between the countries adhering to one or another of these system variations, but also within the various groups inside the same country. These conflicts have had their deleterious effect on the types of industries installed, the locus of capital ownership and control, the criteria used for the success or failure of industrial establishments, the labour policies adopted, and other important aspects of the orientation and operation of industry.

In the third place, there has been considerable questioning in the Arab countries, often suppressed or implicit but no less real, of the relationship between national industry and the international economic system: should industry attempt to retain its independence? Should it allow itself to form rings or links in the strong, far-reaching chain of international industry controlled by the transnational corporations? Can industry acquire the necessary technological capability, finance, and access to markets without linking itself closely to the transnational corporations? Should the Arab countries concern themselves profoundly with questions of dependence on the advanced industrial countries at the present stage when they are taking their first industrial steps, or should they acquire industrial capability first, regardless of the medium or avenue accessible, and attempt independence only later?

Fourthly, the drive for industrialization was plagued by questions regarding the pre-eminence of industry as against agriculture (or some other sector, such as trade) within the context of options available. The questions had far-reaching implications. These related to and impinged strongly on the extent of advantages allowed industry, the clarity (or the fogginess) of the conception of the interrelations and interdependences among the various sectors, the synchromeshing between industrial and educational and training policies.

Finally, industrial development was hampered in part by the indecisiveness of the conceptual and practical answer provided to the question of the technology (or technologies) to be adopted in the various branches of manufacturing industry. This question has many ramifications. The choice of technology is not merely a technical matter. But even at this level it poses many questions with regard to the degree of advancement of technology, the degree of 'appropriateness' of technology, or the aim of industrialization, inasmuch as import-substitution would suggest a technology different from export promotion. On another level, the choice has social and political implications since the 'importation' of technology touches closely on the relations of national economies with the international economic system, but more specifically with the advanced industrial economies (whether market or centrally-planned) and with the transnational companies. In turn, the choice made touches on financing facilities and conditions relating to them; the impact of these on the independence of national industry; the encouragement of the drive for the acquisition of technological capability, and therefore the recourse to design, consultation, engineering, and contracting facilities available in the region itself.

It is necessary to be objective with respect to the need for self-examination relating to these issues, in so far as this is crucial to the assessment of the performance of the industrial sector. Such examination explains the rather unsatisfactory performance of the sector, even by the standards of the Third World in general, let alone those developing countries that have distinguished themselves in this context, both in Latin America and in South and South-east Asia.

6. Money, banking, and public finance

The comparative study of the economies of the Arab region for 1930 and 1980 contained in Part One of this book does not proceed comprehensively, sector by sector, both because in the limited space allowed only the sectors of greater developmental significance can find room and because the non-availability of information for 1930 dictates some exclusions. And, in any case, some chapters do not deal only with economic sectors in the strict sense of the term but also with a few economic factors of significance such as money and public finance, with the overall performance of the economy which transcends sectors, or with Arab economic co-operation and complementarity which transcends individual economies to embrace the whole region.

Money, banking, and public finance are treated together, although they do not constitute one sector or one factor, mainly because of their institutional and functional closeness. While there is inadequate information on each by itself for the early thirties, there is enough to deal with them together, particularly if spot references are made to individual countries which help identify the situation for the region as a whole. As in the cases of industry or land use which have been discussed in earlier chapters, more detailed information for more countries could have been obtained had it not been for the conciseness opted for in this book.

We turn now to the substance of this chapter. Although supportive material is not available, it can be said that the volume of money supply was very small, in the aggregate, compared with what it was by the end of 1979. On the other hand, there is enough information to tell us that the banking system was very small in size and limited in scope in 1930. Five factors have combined to increase considerably the volume of the supply of money and to enlarge and diversify the banking sector. The first is the vast increase in the degree of monetization and of economic sophistication leading to expanded banking operations, as well as increased money supply. In most of the countries now under examination, such as north and south Yemen, Saudi Arabia, the Gulf emirates, Iraq, Syria, Transjordan, Sudan, Libya, Mauritania, and Somalia, large sections of the economies were only slightly monetized in 1930 or thereabouts.

All the banks then in existence were, with few exceptions, foreign-owned (English, French and some Italian) or of mixed ownership, and, in one notable instance, Turkish, going back to the days of Ottoman hegemony. To be specific, in the early thirties only five commercial banks were national (that is, established and controlled by Arab nationals), in addition to four specialized banks – three agricultural and one real estate – all but one of the latter group dating back to Ottoman days. It is very difficult to verify whether the whole capital of all five commercial banks came from Arab nationals, but two of these were definitely all-Arab in ownership: Bank Misr, founded in Cairo in 1920, and the Arab Bank, founded in Jerusalem in 1930. The remaining three were all Lebanese.[48]

It is relevant to state here that, while the three Lebanese banks never grew to be major institutions in banking in the Arab world, Bank Misr and the Arab Bank were to acquire pre-eminence in later years: the first,[49] in actively promoting investment in Egyptian industry and other sectors and itself initiating several important branches. Although essentially a commercial bank, it distinguished itself in undertaking important investments of a developmental nature, and – politically – in breaking the grip of the powerful foreign community in Egypt on banking in the country. Many of the companies that the Bank established came to acquire prominence in later years, down to the present.

However, Bank Misr remained largely restricted to Egypt in its operations. On the other hand, the Arab Bank, although it has remained largely commercial and has not been as active in industrial investment as Bank Misr, has grown considerably both in assets and in regional (and international) coverage. The Arab Bank was the sixth-largest Arab bank in 1979, with \$4 billion of deposits,[50] but it had been the first in 1978. This is a remarkable expansion from the modest beginnings of 1930, when the bank was founded with 15,000 Palestine pounds (sterling pounds) of capital. It is worth noting that the Arab Bank is a private bank, with shareholders from most Arab countries, and it is not based on an oil economy; the five top banks are all focused on oil countries, and three of them are state (nationalized) banks. But for these factors, the Arab Bank would still have the largest volume of deposits among all Arab commercial banks.

The nine top commercial banks with entirely Arab capital may be listed as follows:

Name, Country	*Deposits ($ billion)*
Rafidain Bank, Iraq	8.6
National Commercial Bank, Saudi Arabia	7.0
Banque Nationale d'Algérie, Algeria	6.6
Banque Extérieure d'Algérie, Algeria	6.3
National Bank of Abu Dhabi, United Arab Emirates	4.5
Arab Bank, Jordan	4.0
National Bank of Kuwait, Kuwait	3.3
Al-Ahli Bank, Kuwait	2.8
Gulf Bank, Kuwait	2.1

As well as being few in number and extremely limited in their resources, the banks in 1930 were primitive in their techniques and excessively conservative in outlook. These factors combined with the basic sluggishness of growth of the Arab economies suggest that the banking system played a negligible role in growth and development in the region at large. The notable exception to this generalization is Bank Misr, to which reference has already been made. Within these generalizations, it can be said that the system's operations were felt primarily in the financing of internal commerce and foreign trade, and to a much more limited extent in the agricultural activities of large landowners, inasmuch as there were a number of agricultural banks with several branches in some of the region's countries.

The second reason for the vast increase in the supply of money and the expansion in banking is the overall economic growth that the region has witnessed, along with the marked increase in population. We are not in possession of data to substantiate this assertion, nor would national accounts for the early thirties for all the region's countries be very useful, considering the near-impossibility of making the series of national accounts for the fifty years continuous and acceptable, or of making the value of the different currency units uniform for the whole period. Yet we can safely say, on the strength of several monetary and real indicators, that vast growth has occurred. As a very rough estimate, the aggregate national product per capita of the region has more than quadrupled over the half-century under examination in real terms. Internal commerce and foreign trade have multiplied by a larger factor. Together, economic growth and expansion of trade are a major factor in the expansion of the volume of money supply and of banking institutions and operations.

No less important is the third explanatory factor, which is long-term inflationary trends over the decades since we are dealing here with the money supply in current rather than real terms. A fourth factor is the resort by several countries to deficit-financing, often extensively and for protracted periods. And finally, the fifth factor, expansion in money supply and in the banking sector has been expedited by the formation by most of the Arab governments of specialized banks, such as industrial, agricultural, or development banks. The aggregate capital of these banks stood at the equivalent of $2,807 million by the end of 1979, against aggregate capital accounts totalling $6,697 million for commercial banks, as Table 13 shows.

These five reasons together account for an enormous expansion in the volume of the supply of money, of the banking sector (in terms of number of banks, diversification of banking functions, proliferation of branches, and more widely-spread banking habits), and of banking operations. Table 14 shows the money supply by the end of 1979 (defined as comprising currency outside banks and private sector's demand deposits in banks) to be equivalent to $82,927 million. In conclusion, it can be said that the volume of money supply cannot but be tens of times as large as it was in 1930, while the capital of commercial and specialized banks is today probably larger than it was in 1930 by a more sizeable factor. The exact volumes being compared are not as significant as may appear on the surface; it is enough in the present context to recognize

TABLE 13

Arab banks: capital accounts of commercial banks and capital of specialized banks, 1979 ([a])
(million US dollars) ([b])

Country	Capital accounts ([c]) commercial banks	Capital specialized banks ([d])
Iraq	304.4	694.2
Kuwait	972.4	409.3
Saudi Arabia	758.7	995.3
Bahrain	90.9	–
Qatar	102.2	88.5
UAE	1,193.2	144.7
Oman	39.7	51.8
Yemen A.R.	87.9	–
P.D.R. Yemen	19.9	–
Jordan	225.9	83.2
Syria	135.5	76.6
Lebanon	270.8	18.5
Egypt	1,101.5	60.0
Sudan	49.7	94.2 ([e])
Libya	397.6	–
Tunisia	210.8	31.8
Algeria	558.8	26.0
Morocco	157.2	33.2
Mauritania	17.9	–
Somalia	2.3	–
Total	6,697.3	2,807.3

Notes:

([a]) Except for Iraq, 1976; Algeria and Morocco, 1978.

([b]) Conversion from national currencies at *IFS* rates.

([c]) Including capital and reserves.

([d]) Data here are of lower reliability than for commercial banks.

([e]) Excluding the Arab Bank for Economic Development in Africa (a regional bank with headquarters in Sudan), the Arab Authority for Agricultural Investment and Development (another regional agency), and the Sudan Authority for Development. Their aggregate capital is $1,200 million.

Sources: (1) For commercial banks, International Monetary Fund, *International Financial Statistics*, April 1981, except for Egypt (Central Bank of Egypt, *Economic Review*, vol. 19, No. 3/4, 1979; Algeria and Morocco (*Bankers' Almanac & Year Book*, 1980–81). (2) For specialized banks, Union of Arab Banks, *Directory of Arab Banks* (Beirut; in Arabic), and *The Middle East and North Africa, 1979–80* (Europa Publications, London).

the indicators which firmly suggest the vast expansion in both instances.

The greater significance of these magnitudes lies in their relevance to the financing of development. They show that the Arab region has acquired much greater liquidity with which to finance development projects and programmes as well as consumption needs and imports. Yet this is insufficient explanation of the financial capabilities of the Arab region today, in view of the fact that its aggregate GDP for 1979 stood at about the equivalent of $300 billion, or that the aggregate investment allocations in the development plans of eighteen of the region's countries totalled $326 billion for the period 1975–80. The money supply and the capital accounts of the commercial and specialized banks together fall far short of serving as the financial medium for the annual flows called for by aggregate GDP and development allocations of the volume indicated.

The gap is filled by bank credit, which, obviously, is much more substantial than the aggregate capital accounts of the banking system in its entirety. Herein lies the fundamental point about the role of money and banking in promoting development. It is that they serve as a 'lubricating' medium, one which was of extremely minor significance in the early thirties, but whose size and improved performance render it highly contributive now. However, this requires appropriate and sound policies, in the monetary, fiscal, and banking areas, economic, technical, and institutional in nature. And the most relevant of these policies are those that aim at the promotion of development.

Yet, in spite of the relevance and significance of all these policy areas, they cannot be discussed here: they require the spread of the discussion over all the sectors and main activities, and, further, over such matters as import and export policies, pricing policies, foreign exchange policies, discount and interest rate policies – to name just a few. It will not be possible to discuss this important aspect of economic change in the region, with its twenty-one states, for a period of fifty years. We will therefore have to limit ourselves to the consequences of these policies, and of many others outside money, banking, and public finance, with respect to development.

TABLE 14

Arab countries: money supply, end 1979 ([a])

Country	Money supply millions of national currency	Money supply millions of US dollars
Iraq (1977)	1,785.2	6,045
Kuwait	669.4	2,425
Saudi Arabia	54,700.0	16,276
Bahrain	217.5	568
Qatar	2,491.6	658
UAE	6,269.0	1,650
Oman	123.2	357
Yemen A.R.	7,036.9	1,542
P.D.R. Yemen	184.9	535
Jordan	465.6	1,549
Syria	16,010.0	4,053
Lebanon	6,684.0	2,061
Egypt	4,354.2	10,462
Sudan	836.5	1,969
Libya (1978)	1,727.5	5,835
Tunisia	785.8	1,925
Algeria	71,421.0	18,535
Morocco	23,508.0	6,000
Mauritania	5,081.0	111
Somalia	2,335.3	371
Total		82,927

Note:
([a]) Comprising currency outside banks and private sector's demand deposits.

Source: International Monetary Fund, *International Financial Statistics*, September 1980.

The last chapter, however, will attempt to probe deeper into the definition and exploration of the main issues of Arab development, and, in so doing, will touch on some policy aspects of these issues.

Public finance will be studied in the present chapter since, together with money and banking operations, it reflects and services economic activity in general. Early in the thirties, the resources at the disposal of the Arab treasuries or the ministries of finance (and through these, at the disposal of the various government ministries and departments) were mostly directed towards the financing of the current operations of government – salaries and wages of the employees of public authorities,

TABLE 15

Comparison of government revenues and expenditures in 1930 and 1979: selected Arab countries

Country	Millions of national currency 1930 Revenues	Millions of national currency 1930 Expenditures	Millions of national currency 1979 Revenues	Millions of national currency 1979 Expenditures	Millions of US dollars 1979 Revenues	Millions of US dollars 1979 Expenditures
Iraq	3.5	3.8	9,467	9,467	32,058	32,058
Kuwait	—	—	2,301	1,950	8,264	7,004
Bahrain	—	—	280	280	726	726
Saudi Arabia	—	—	130,000	130,000	38,298	38,298
Yemen A.R.	—	—	3,013	4,384	661	961
Jordan (Transjordan)	0.4	0.4	401	513	1,347	1,722
Syria (a)	11.1	10.9	22,641	22,641	5,769	5,769
Lebanon (a)	5.3	5.3	1,806	2,806	549	853
Egypt	38.6	41.2	10,249	12,929	15,116	19,069
Tunisia (b)	200.0	200.0	625	625	1,520	1,520
Algeria (c)	720.0	720.0	36,901	36,881	9,635	9,630
Morocco (d)	450.0	450.0	19,078	19,477	4,579	4,674

Notes:

(a) Figures for Lebanon and Syria for 1930 are quoted in LSL (Syrian Lebanese pounds) which were then interchangeable.

(b) The currency base for 1979 for Tunisia is the dinar, whose relationship to the 1930 franc is different from that of the Algerian dinar or the Moroccan dirham.

(c) Old 1930 francs for Algeria and Morocco were converted to 1979 units at the rate of 100 to 1.

(d) For Morocco, the latest data refer to 1978, not 1979.

Sources: For Mashreq countries in 1930, sources in Note 1. For Maghreb countries, Samir Amin, op. cit., pp. 48 ff. For 1979, *The Middle East and North Africa, 1979–80*, already referred to.

rents of government offices, and other recurrent expenditures. Allocations of a developmental or capital nature were a small proportion of total government expenditure. On the whole, the capital budget went into public works – the building of roads and bridges, schools and hospitals, and irrigation canals and networks. Taken together, the region's countries allocated around 10 or 12 per cent of total budget expenditure to capital investment – with the (then) poorer countries allocating less than the lower of these two figures.[51] The remainder of the budget went into recurrent expenditures.

The overall size of the total budgets was itself very modest half a century ago. This statement is based on a crude comparison between the volume of revenues and expenditures in 1930 and in 1979/80, which can be made in the case of a small number of countries, as Table 15 shows. The table records values in terms of current prices, that is, without taking into account the drop in the value of money, whether through official devaluation or inflation; economic growth and increase in population over the decades which, in themselves, call for expansion in the supply of money, credit, and public finance; or the vast expansion in the powers and responsibilities of Arab governments since 1930, including the emergence of a very large public sector in several instances – an expansion which has occasioned substantially increased expenditure and therefore the mobilization of substantially increased revenues. In combination, these factors have led to a very steep rise in government expenditure for eight countries for which data are available – the current budgets being more than 40 times larger than the 1930 budget at the minimum, and over 2,400 times at the maximum.

There are two aspects of particular significance for the examination of public finance in the context of development. The first is the considerably enlarged role of government in the design, control, financing, and execution of development work. This role has changed qualitatively as well as quantitatively. The entry of government into the economic sphere as a whole has become direct and active: gone are the shyness and apologetic hesitation of the past. Furthermore, the role of government has evolved from concentrating on the provision of an appropriate climate for private investment (legislation, law and order, credit facilities, infrastructure), to one involving first the establishment of projects, then whole programmes, and finally overall planning for the whole economy whether or not the private sector still retains a wide field for its activity. Planning, and the control of resources in general, has become accepted and pursued, irrespective of ideological orientation and socio-economic philosophy.

Quantitatively, the size of the national development plans of the various countries has acquired considerable magnitude. The aggregate of planned investment in eighteen Arab states for the period 1975–80 totalled the equivalent of $326 billion, as already stated. The total for the five years 1981–5, judging by the plans already published, promises to be considerably larger. Even given the discrepancy between planned and actual investment, which could well be 30 per cent of investment plans, the volume involved is still substantial. As the bulk of the investment planned is designed to be made by government and the public sector, the magnitude and role of public finance will be appreciated from this indicator alone, apart from the vast growth of recurrent expenditures and other indicators.

Taken together, recurrent and capital expenditure for 1979 totalled about $160 billion for the Arab states, excluding Djibouti.[52] Capital investment allocations for 1979 (which, as one-fifth of the aggregate for five years of $326 billion average 65 billion) amount to 40 per cent of the aggregate combined budgets. Related to GDP, the overall budgets stood at 53 per cent, while budgeted investment stood at 23 per cent. Actual investment effected, estimating it to have fallen below the plans by 30 per cent, would be $46 billion or 15.3 per cent of GDP. To this must be added investment made by the private sector, estimated in the aggregate to be in the region of $41 billion. The public sector (including government proper) and the private sector are estimated to have together effected some $87.5 billion of investment,[53] or about 29 per cent of aggregate GDP. Such a volume of investment could account for a rate of growth of 8 or 9 per cent, which would be in line with information and estimates relating to the economic performance of the Arab region as a whole for the year 1979.

The second point of significance in the present context is that by far the largest single source of finance to meet the recurrent and capital expenditures under the aggregated budgets has been oil revenues. The social and economic implications of the heavy dependence on the oil sector will be examined in the last chapter, as one of the major issues of Arab development. It will be sufficient at this point to state that oil revenue does not arise from the generation of income by a renewable resource, but from the sale and depletion of a non-renewable resource. Furthermore, oil revenue apart, indirect taxes constitute a much larger source of public revenue than direct taxes, both personal and corporate. Indeed, the returns of income and capital taxes are either non-existent with respect to the nationals of some of the oil-exporting countries, or else they bring in negligible revenue – indeed, in certain cases, a shrinking proportion of all tax revenue, always excluding oil revenue. The serious implications of this state of dependence on oil must be emphasized, although the resort to oil revenues for the financing of developmental investment is understandable and justifiable in itself. The justification is that oil revenues are used in large part to build up the productive capabilities of the oil-producing countries, so that they can substitute for oil revenues when these become negligible or disappear.

What is not justifiable is the 'exemption' of the beneficiaries of development, who are capable of doing so, from shouldering a fair part of the financial obligations both of development efforts and of social services. If it does not seem necessary now, or for a decade or two, to tax the citizens of the oil-exporting countries, it will certainly prove very necessary after the high level of oil revenues begins to slope downwards and society finds that it has to work hard to generate a national product which will provide as credible a substitute for the revenues as possible.

7. External economic relations

The Arab region has had rather intensive relations with the West for centuries now. Its geographical location, stretched as it is around the Mediterranean, its accessibility and its easy access to Europe, Asia, and Africa, the Arab/Islamic meteoric burst into the world, both east and west, with all that this signified in cultural and economic interaction – have all been factors that forbade isolation and made for long-standing economic intercourse with the outside world. But if the centuries of Ottoman hegemony meant a greater inwardness of economic relations at the expense of relations with countries outside the vast reach of the Ottoman empire, the strong European drive for colonization in the nineteenth and twentieth centuries brought about a restructuring of relations.

This drive put the resources, location, markets, communications, and manpower of the region under the control of the European powers whose industrialization process had then taken off vigorously, or was in its early take-off phase. The relationship that ensued was one of exploitation by those powers – an exploitation which, in its economic confines took the form of manufactured exports to the region and raw material imports from it, along with the use of the location and the communication potential and facilities of the region, basically to the advantage of the colonial powers.

The economic relations did not, of course, take shape and substance in a vacuum, but were conducted within a context that included political/military and cultural aspects. The political/military aspect provided the base for power and authority, and of course the element of coercion essential to the 'colonialist enterprise'. The cultural aspect unfolded in two ways: the first indirect, spurred on by the contacts between colonizer and colonized, travel, and a general, if restricted, observation of Europe; the second direct, through deliberate efforts by the colonial powers to influence the education, thinking, and behaviour of the colonized – mainly through mission schools and printed matter. But in the final analysis, whatever the point of tangency and the means and field of contact, whether political, military, or cultural, the objective was the uncovering, consolidation, and exploitation of economic interests, either perceived through the narrow context of the parties directly concerned, or through the much wider context of the colonial power's global network of interests.

In their turn, economic relations took several forms, including trade; the exploitation of resources and the establishment by foreign interests of public utilities and certain industries – usually under concessionary terms; the 'colonization' of agricultural land; the building of roads, railways, and ports; and the setting-up of banks. But the form or component of these relations which will occupy us here is trade. Financial flows were not unimportant, especially in those Arab countries which were colonies and not under 'mandate', such as the Maghreb countries (including Libya). The flows that would be of special interest in this context are budgetary support and other payments made necessary by the presence of occupation forces and foreign personnel in the civil service, as well as by investments required for the modern (colonial) economy. It is not, however, possible within the narrow scope of this chapter to undertake the necessary research into these flows; the discussion will therefore deal primarily with trade in the earlier part of the period with which we are concerned, but will widen to include trade and aid flows in later years. The aid flows now move in two directions: inwards from the industrial countries, and outwards from the Arab oil-exporting countries.

Imports and exports of commodities and services have shown a vast growth, both in volume and in value, over the five decades under examination. The reasons behind such growth have been touched upon in the context of the discussion of money supply, banking operations, and public budgets, and we need only enumerate them here as a reminder. They are population increase and economic growth, greater diversification and sophistication of the economies, intensification of development efforts, expansion in consumption and changes in consumption habits, and erosion in the purchasing power of money.

These long-term trends are a matter of common knowledge, but to substantiate the statements more concrete quantitative information is needed than is readily available for several of the region's countries. We are therefore forced, once again, to make spot references to the foreign trade of a small number of countries for which data for the thirties are available. These references will be sufficient to show the vast expansion in the value of imports and exports when seen against the value for 1979, a year for which foreign trade data are available.

The countries for which comparison is possible, thanks to the similarity of the currency unit used (disregarding here the

TABLE 16

Commodity imports and exports for selected countries 1930s and 1979 (millions of national currency)

Country	Year	Commodity imports	Commodity exports
Egypt	1930	47.5	31.9
	1979	2,686.0	1,287.8
Syria and Lebanon	1931	50.5	12.0
Syria	1979	13,067.0	6,453.0
Lebanon	1979	7,248.0	2,285.0
Transjordan	1936	0.9	0.2
Jordan (East Bank)	1979	589.5	120.9
Iraq	1930/31	5.4	3.1 (*a*)
	1979	2,224.9	6,349.8
Tunisia	1930 (*b*)	310.0	390.0
	1979	1,169.0	975.0
Algeria	1930 (*b*)	1,270.0	1,270.0
	1979	28,900.0	31,556.0
Morocco	1930 (*b*)	720.0	230.0
	1979	14,328.0	7,287.0

Notes:

(*a*) Excluding oil.

(*b*) For the Maghreb countries the currency used is 1930 francs at 1955 values (as in the source; see Note 54). In the case of Tunisia, 350 francs at 1955 value were equal to one dinar (which was to be introduced in 1958 as the new currency unit, at the rate of 0.42 dinar to one US dollar).

Sources: Varied; see Note 54.

change in the purchasing power, or value, of the currency), are Egypt, Syria and Lebanon (whose trade reporting was combined in the thirties), Transjordan (currently known as the East Bank of the Hashemite Kingdom of Jordan), and Iraq in the Mashreq; and Tunisia, Algeria, and Morocco in the Maghreb. In Table 16 we list the value of their commodity imports and exports for the early thirties and for 1979 in their national currencies. (Data on invisibles – the imports and exports of services – are not available for 1930.) The enormous contrast between the foreign trade of the early thirties and that of 1979 is immediately apparent from the table.[54]

The contrast between foreign trade in the thirties and that in 1979 becomes much greater once imports and exports of non-factor services are included in the 1979 data, since these too have grown enormously in value beyond their base in 1930. This is known in general terms, and can be surmised from a number of relevant indicators. The overall picture of foreign trade (including services) in 1979 can be seen and appreciated in Table 17, in which the national currencies have been converted into US dollars. As Table 17 shows, total imports aggregated for the region amount to $111.7 billion, while total exports amount to $169.2 billion. The latter include oil exports.[55]

Two observations will be made here with respect to the comparison between commodity imports and exports over the fifty-year stretch, before a look is taken at the region's foreign trade in 1979 by itself, and its implications at both the national and the regional levels. The first relates to the composition of foreign trade in the early thirties and in the late seventies. For Egypt, by far the largest class of imports was textile materials and textiles, followed distantly by vegetable products; chemical and pharmaceutical products; mineral products; food, beverages, and tobacco; metals and metal articles; and machinery, apparatus, and electrical materials. Together these accounted for some 88 per cent of total imports. Three classes of exports accounted for 89 per cent of the total; all three appear under the prominent import classes, namely, textile materials and textiles, vegetable products, and food, beverages, and tobacco. On the other hand, the value of machinery and intermediate and capital goods exports in general is signally insignificant.

It is noticeable that the major import classes of Syria and Lebanon in 1931 were identical with those in Egypt, accounting for about 67 per cent of total imports. And the same is more or less true of the composition of exports, where the same major classes accounted for 80 per cent of the total. One difference in the pattern of imports is that there is less concentration on classes in Syria and Lebanon except in textiles and textile materials. This greater diffusion can also be seen in Iraq, where textiles and common metals, which are by far the leading import classes, together account for only 43 per cent of total imports. But vegetable products and textiles, which form the major export classes, accounted in the thirties for 83 per cent of the total for Iraq.

As a general observation it can be stated that in the case of both imports and exports, but especially the latter, the goods entering foreign trade were mostly consumers' and intermediate goods, not capital goods. But whereas the imports as a rule included a large proportion of manufactured goods, the exports included a large proportion of raw materials and other goods in an early stage of production.

In contrast, imports and exports for 1979 contain more sophisticated goods, particularly the imports. These also include a much higher proportion of capital goods and intermediate goods to be used as inputs for further investment, under the strong pressure of the drive for development. The range of exports, on the other hand, is narrow. Indeed, oil exports apart, the region's economies seem to be characterized by a narrowing of the range of exports, except in a few countries. The most prominent exceptions are Egypt and Lebanon, particularly the former; Egypt used to depend heavily on cotton and textiles but now has a noticeably larger range of exports, while Lebanon has always had a wider range of exports, by regional standards. Again, apart from oil, the new export classes include building materials, electrical materials and appliances, furniture, printed materials, glass, pharmaceuticals and petroleum products, food products (more sophisticated than in the past), textiles, and some machines and equipment.

But the most outstanding feature of exports in 1979 is the pre-eminence of petroleum and other minerals in the region's total exports. Roughly speaking, oil alone accounts for over 90 per cent of total Arab exports, while oil, phosphates, and other minerals account for 95 per cent. These proportions become larger if the countries exporting oil and other minerals are considered alone. The serious implications of this high level of export concentration will be examined later.

The second observation to be made with respect to foreign trade relates to the source of imports and the destination of exports. In the thirties trade with other Arab countries was very small for the countries that are surveyed here, both in imports and in exports. Only in the case of Syria and Lebanon did it constitute a noticeable proportion; some 10 per cent of imports, but over 45 per cent of exports. In both Egypt and Iraq it was well below 5 per cent. It is a condemnation of the sluggishness of Arab regional trade that today, some fifty years later, trade among the countries of the region is still restricted within a narrow range of 6–7 per cent for both imports and exports. The situation is rather different, however, with respect to the rest of the world. The advanced industrial countries still dominate the region's foreign trade, whether as suppliers or as markets for goods (and for services, for that matter). But, whereas in the early thirties only Egypt had some modest trade with the Soviet Union in 1930 (but none in the rest of the decade), today the Soviet Union and the other socialist countries feature more importantly as trading partners. Although a number of Arab countries have no, or only very insignificant trade with the socialist countries, some, such as Sudan and Egypt, rely quite appreciably on them in their exports.

On comparing the socialist countries as a group with the group of OECD countries, we find that the latter accounts for well over two-thirds of the Arab region's imports and exports, while the remaining third is accounted for by trade within the region, with other Third World countries, and with the socialist group. This pattern represents a decline for the socialist group from the sixties, when trade with it featured much more prominently. The decline can be attributed both to political and ideological shifts in the seventies and to the steep rise in the absolute and relative importance of oil exports, which has increased the dealings with OECD countries much more than those with the socialist countries. It has done so directly in the case of exports but also indirectly in the case of imports, in the sense that much of the oil exports to Western countries go to finance imports from them.[56]

Two aspects of the region's external economic relations were stated earlier in this chapter to occupy the centre of attention: trade and aid flows, but primarily the first. So far, only trade has been discussed. But before we examine the aid flows, both within the region and between it and other regions, we need to take a closer look at the implications of the vast growth of Arab foreign trade and the composition of exports and imports. For this purpose Table 17 presents the value of the exports and imports of the Arab countries for the year 1979, and five implications will be identified and assessed.

It is regrettable that no comparable identification and assessment is possible of the implications of the size and composition of foreign trade for the year 1930 or the early thirties, owing to insufficient detail in trade statistics for the period. Nevertheless, it can be stated that the current situation is qualitatively different from that in the early thirties, not just quantitatively, although the quantitative differences are so enormous as to be in effect of qualitative significance themselves also. The size and pre-eminence of the oil sector – a phenomenon of the seventies for which there is no parallel in the thirties – and the fact that the disturbing implications to be examined are encountered even though the region's countries are now politically independent, whereas in 1930 only two of them were independent, together constitute grounds for distinct qualitative differentiation. The magnitude of the change in the value of foreign trade only accentuates this differentiation.

1. The first implication of the pattern and volume of foreign trade in 1979 is that trade puts vastly increased resources at the disposal of the economies. The resources become available in two ways: through the increase in the national product of the various countries – particularly in

the oil-producing countries, and through the excess of imports over exports (the 'import surplus'), which is financed through economic aid coming in from outside the states concerned, and/or the drawing-down of financial reserves, or the increase of foreign indebtedness. The compensatory

TABLE 17

Foreign trade of the Arab countries, 1979 (a)
(million US dollars) (b)

Country	Exports (c) Total ($m.)	Exports (c) Per capita (e) ($)	Imports (d) Total ($m.)	Imports (d) Per capita (e) ($)
Iraq	21,448.5	1,662.7	12,382.3	959.9
Kuwait	18,295.5	14,259.9	4,933.4	3,845.2
Saudi Arabia	64,324.9	7,844.5	29,225.8	3,564.1
Bahrain	2,403.8	6,829.0	2,281.3	6,481.0
Qatar	3,576.7	16,871.2	1,420.3	6,700.9
UAE	14,253.5	18,730.0	5,910.0	7,766.1
Oman	2,160.4	2,477.5	1,284.0	1,472.5
Yemen A.R.	263.7	44.9	1,666.1	283.8
P.D.R. Yemen	111.8	58.2	405.3	211.1
Jordan	932.2	309.4	2,064.4	685.2
Syria	1,750.9	206.7	3,266.3	385.6
Lebanon (f)	701.5	224.8	2,225.0	712.9
Egypt	8,318.4	200.9	12,837.9	310.1
Sudan	744.6	41.0	1,322.8	72.9
Libya	15,926.3	5,491.8	10,741.4	3,703.9
Tunisia	2,387.9	369.6	2,863.1	443.2
Algeria	8,550.3	440.7	11,557.6	595.7
Morocco	2,736.6	138.6	4,640.4	234.9
Mauritania	188.2	117.2	406.6	253.2
Somalia	134.2	37.5	308.1	86.1
Total	169,209.9		111,742.4	
(Average)		(1,056.2)		(697.5)

Notes:
(a) Exluding Djibouti.
(b) Rates of conversion from national currencies to US dollars are those listed in source of foreign trade data.
(c) Exports include goods and non-factor services.
(d) Imports include goods and non-factor services.
(e) Per capita calculations are based on population data in Table 1.
(f) Goods only.

Sources: Arab Fund National Accounts Country Tables for exports and imports in national currencies, conversion to US dollars by the author, and calculation of per capita exports and imports by the author.

factor is reflected in the balance of payment of the region's countries.[57]

In the latter connection, it must be noted that the region shows a surplus on current account in its aggregate balance of payments for 1979, of over $57 billion, thanks to the oil exports of a number of countries. Yet not all oil producers and exporters have a surplus: indeed, only eight countries ended with a surplus, as Table 17 shows. (Remittances from nationals working abroad in such countries of the region as Egypt, Yemen Arab Republic, PDRY, Lebanon, Syria, and Jordan are factor services and are an important additional component in the current accounts of the balances of payments of those countries. In the same way, remittances from Tunisians, Moroccans, and Algerians working in Europe constitute an important addition.)

It is pertinent in the present context that the vast expansion in available resources permits the allocation of greatly increased resources to both consumption and capital formation (that is, investment in development work). Both uses of resources will be examined in the following chapter, but some of their aspects will be examined here.

2. The consumption patterns that have emerged in what we may call the recent oil era of the seventies have a serious implication which is reflected in the data of foreign trade. Total consumption in the region amounted to $160 billion for 1979. It is a coincidence that this figure is identical with that of the market value of oil produced in the region; nevertheless it is a disturbing coincidence, in that it highlights the fast, undisciplined increase in consumption (particularly in the oil-exporting countries). Not only is the total value of resources directed to consumption a matter for concern but also the pattern of consumption that is emerging, with the growing component of imported goods (and services) for consumption, and, among these, the large component of luxury or less necessary goods (and services). While allowing for the pressure of pent-up demand, and the impact of imitation and the 'demonstration effect' in this pattern, it still remains a source of anxiety, especially as it becomes entrenched and therefore difficult to alter in the future.

3. The third feature of the composition of imports is the

relatively large category of capital goods imported, as well as technical services for developmental uses. There is here a creditable implication, and it is worth encouraging. Nevertheless, there is urgent need for greater discretion in the design of development plans and programmes; a proper system of priorities should be established that would take into account the more significant objectives of development. It hardly needs to be said that while superficially all investment can be considered developmental in nature, a more searching examination may establish a hierarchy in the urgency and relevance of different development programmes and projects. This is particularly important in the present case because the bulk of the flow of imports is possible only because of the export of oil, a most valuable but non-renewable natural resource.

4. The ratio of imports and exports combined to GDP is rising fast and constitutes a growing form of dependency on the external sector. Thus, while imports plus exports constituted 60 per cent of GDP in 1970, they rose to 88 per cent in 1978, and to about 92 per cent in 1979.[58] Of greater significance, however, is the ratio of imports plus exports to GDP if the oil exports were to be excluded from GDP. This ratio is 179:100, that is, imports plus exports would then exceed GDP by 79 per cent. In the absence of oil exports the whole picture would obviously change, both for imports and for exports. The exercise just conducted is none the less useful in highlighting the heavy dependence on oil exports, and how this dependence may lead to very dangerous permissiveness in imports. A by-product of this situation is that oil-exporting countries with larger populations and more varied resources (such as Iraq, Saudi Arabia, Libya, and Algeria) would have been forced, if they had not had oil, to encourage production and export in other sectors, instead of allowing the high concentration that we now witness in production and exports. A result of this concentration is the leakage which the fast-growing imports represent. Thus the significantly increased purchasing power, particularly in the oil-exporting countries, is inadequately reflected in expanded and diversified production inside the region. Instead, a disproportionate part of it leaks out in the form of imports.

5. This form of leakage has another aspect: increased dependence on the advanced industrial countries. This dependence is reflected in various areas, but it it manifest also in that of foreign trade, with regard to both goods and services. Obviously, the resort to importation, particularly of non-essential goods and services or of those capable of being produced in the region, is the outward manifestation of dependence. The root of this dependence is the attitude of mind that tends to attach priority to foreign goods and services and to reduce the will to replace them by means of national and regional efforts and productive capabilities. The fact that these capabilities might be glaringly short in many areas of commodity production and technical, professional, and administrative skills must be treated as a challenge for diversification, improvement, and expansion in production and economic/technical performance in general.

To refer to the shortage as a challenge is to stress the vital urgency of joint Arab action aimed at economic complementarity. More will be said about regional co-operation and complementarity in Chapter 9. It is necessary at this point to state that self-reliant development is only possible at the regional level, that is, the global Arab level, and that such development is essential if the excessive dependence on the advanced industrial world and its transnational corporations is to be effectively corrected. Obviously, the economic/technological dependence has far-reaching politico-strategic implications.

The present chapter has been designed to deal with economic aid, in addition to foreign trade, as major aspects of the external sector. Some brief observations will be made with respect to aid, particularly Arab aid deployed within the region, since more will be said on this subject in Chapter 9.

Until the end of 1973 the region received much more economic aid (in the form of loans of varying duration, and some grants either in cash or in the form of technical assistance) from outside the region than from inside. If we take the four decades up to the early seventies together, the bulk of the aid will be found to have come from Western Europe and the United States, although from the second half of the fifties until the end of the sixties the Soviet Union and the other socialist countries also emerged as significant donors and distinguished themselves by offering their aid mainly in the form of goods and services for the establishment of infrastructural and directly productive projects. Irrespective of source, foreign aid in the post-war period preceding the new oil era, that is, 1945–74, amounted in the aggregate to about one-fourth of gross investment in the Arab region, or some 4 per cent of the average GDP in the reference period. It will be remembered that GDP had not yet reached the very high level of the late seventies, being some $39 billion in 1970 and some $69 billion for 1973 (as against some $300 billion for 1979).[59] Since 1974 the picture has changed fundamentally: aid from Arab oil-exporting countries has become much more significant than non-Arab aid, and by the late seventies stood at some $4–5 billion a year on average. In comparison, non-Arab aid had begun to look almost marginal until 1978 and 1979, when the United States raised its aid to Egypt considerably as a result of the signature by Egypt of a peace treaty with Israel. (Aid to Egypt averaged about $1 billion for the three years 1978–80.) But, considerable as Arab aid has become, it remains well below the urgent needs of the capital-short countries and of the financing capacity of the capital-surplus countries.

The record of the oil-exporting countries in aid-giving has been commendable since 1974, taken on a global basis and considering all forms and avenues of aid. These include government-to-government aid, aid through the national and regional funds (the Arab Fund for Economic and Social Development, AFESD, and the Arab Monetary Fund, AMF), credits opened in favour of certain governments or public institutions, aid through the OPEC Fund for International Development, or through facilities extended by the oil-exporters to the World Bank and the International Monetary Fund. Nevertheless, when the reserves accumulating in Western money markets are taken into account, we can see that there is wide scope for substantial additional aid for development in the Arab region, on both a national (country) and a regional basis.

It is necessary to recall, at this point, that total net official development assistance, ODA, from OPEC countries to the Third World in general and to multilateral institutions, for the six years 1974–79, amounted to $45.5 billion, and that Arab aid by itself (from OAPEC countries) amounted to 90 per cent of the total, or $41 billion. As against this, net official disbursements of ODA by OECD countries for the same period amounted to $93.7 billion.[60] OECD aid amounted to 69.6 per cent of ODA for the years 1974–9, while that of OAPEC countries accounted for 30.4 per cent.

The contrast is striking. The aggregate GDP for the whole Arab region was $300 billion for 1979, or less than the GDP of Italy alone for the same year, which stood at about $334 billion. (Aggregate GNP of OECD countries for 1979 is reported by the *World Development Report, 1980*, as being $6.5 trillion, that is, $6,500 thousand billion.) Furthermore, if related to GDP, Arab aid is over 10 times as large a percentage as that of OECD countries which stood at 0.34 per cent of GNP for 1979, but many times larger still if the calculation is made only for the donor members of OAPEC. When considered within the context of Arab requirements and capabilities, however, Arab aid looks much less impressive.

8. Overall economic performance and structure

The acid test of the progress made over the years in the sectors to which reference has been made in earlier chapters, as well in all other sectors, but particularly those directly relevant to development, such as construction and building, and transport and communications, is the ability of the economy to produce those goods and services needed and wanted by the society or, at least, to produce a large number of these and be able to export some of its excess production for the purchase of varieties not produced internally. The ability in question is measured by what have come to be known as the 'national accounts', which are presented as tables of national income, gross national product, and gross domestic product. In addition, the balance of payments as part of these accounts presents the picture of the economy's earnings and payments (or the inflows into it and the outflows from it) of foreign currencies.

An examination of the progress made in the economies of the Arab region will be undertaken in the present chapter via an examination of the national accounts. Later in the chapter the identification of the structure of the economies as it has developed over the decades, and of the main factors making for change in that structure, will also be attempted.

National accounting is a fairly recent addition to the major tools of the economists; in the early thirties no Arab country had national accounts prepared, although estimates were made later for Palestine, Egypt, and the Maghreb countries (Tunisia, Algeria, and Morocco).[61] The earliest national accounts for Lebanon go back to the years 1948–50; those for Jordan to 1950; those for Iraq to 1952; and those for Syria to 1953.[62] The other countries were to wait several years before they had national account estimates.

The estimates for the several countries listed related to different years, followed different methodologies, and had widely divergent degrees of coverage and reliability. They cannot, therefore, be aggregated or even compared effectively. On the other hand, national accounting is currently undertaken in almost all the countries of the region, and the accounts can be put in a form that permits comparison and aggregation, thanks to the efforts of the World Bank and the International Monetary Fund, as well as the Arab Fund for Economic and Social Development, and the Arab Monetary Fund. Each of the last two agencies has national account Country Tables for the years 1970–9, and we have relied on these tables as our source in this chapter.

Without data capable of permitting a comparison of economic performance between 1930 and 1979 or 1980 for the region's countries, the student of development has to look for alternative courses, in order to assess the extent and quality of the social and economic change that the region has witnessed. One of the few courses theoretically available is to examine the level of living which the economic performance permitted in 1930 against that permitted today. But here again, research, however careful and painstaking, would be unable to reveal all the particulars required: calorie and protein intake; clothing and housing conditions; electricity and other energy consumption per head; education and health facilities available. employment opportunities and degree of fullness of employment enjoyed. Even if information were available; in general terms, it would not tell us much about the actual *distribution* of the goods, services, facilities, and opportunities involved among social and economic groups. As averages are notoriously deceptive, this course must be discarded, even if research were possible and data available. (The pattern of distribution of income and wealth is impossible to define even for 1979, except in the most general terms.)

The student of development is thus left without a scientifically acceptable course. There is, however, one procedure which might enable us to appreciate the extent and quality of change experienced over the fifty years under consideration, 1930–80. This is a mixture of observation of physcial change (food, clothing, housing, energy consumption, education, and health); components of national accounts wherever available; and 'enlightened guesswork'. The last part of the procedure is based essentially on the notion of what could have been achieved over the fifty years, given the levels of education and technology, the resource endowments, and the extent and effectiveness of their exploitation. Thus, this would suggest that the national product per head in real terms could not have risen at a rate permitting more than a quadrupling in the five decades under examination, except for the very steep rise in oil revenues in the last six years of the seventies. It is easy to estimate the direct effect of this rise on the national product for the period 1974 to 1979, but the multiplier and indirect effects would be virtually impossible to calculate, in view of the many complicating factors that enter the picture – nationally, regionally, and internationally. Nevertheless, oil revenues in the period 1974–9 must have permitted a five- or sixfold rise in national product per head, instead of a fourfold rise between 1930 and 1980.

Yet, for the national product in real terms to quadruple, or even to rise by five or six times, in fifty years would still not explain the transformation of national income for Egypt from, say, *£E* 185 million in 1935 (or 157 million for 1939) to a GDP of 9,860 million at factor cost for 1979, no matter how tentative the 1935 or 1939 estimate is. A fuller explanation must of course take into account the net increase in population and the deterioration in the value of money over the years. The same applies to the Maghreb countries, for which data refer back to 1930. (In this subregion, GDP at market prices for 1979 ranges between 19 and 25 times what it had been in 1930 (at 1955 values), according to Samir Amin's calculations.)

If nothing much can be gained in specific terms from such comparisons, at least it is possible to examine the level of performance reached in 1979. Three tables enable us to look at the year 1979 in detail and also to make comparisons between 1970 and 1979. This ten-year period brought a more dramatic change than any earlier decade had witnessed, with GDP at factor cost and at current prices for 1979 standing at 7.7 times what it had been for 1970, that is, $300,678.2 million as against $38,938.8 million. (If inflation is taken into account, the ratio will drop to 2.5 or 3 times. But on a per capita basis, the rise would be 2 to 2.3 times.)

Tables 18, 19, and 20 also enable us, subsequently, to examine the structure of the region's economies and the changes in this structure over the decade.

Obviously, the steep rise in GDP for the oil-exporting countries, and the more moderate rise for the oil-producing countries in general, in the main accounts for this rise. This is clear from the fact that the oil exporters accounted in 1970 for $20,330.4 million or 52.2 per cent of the aggregate GDP for the region ($29,976.9 million or 77 per cent for all 12 oil-producing countries), but the seven oil-exporting countries accounted for $227,716.1 million representing 75.7 per cent of aggregate GDP in 1979 ($272,406.3 million or 90.6 per cent for the oil-producing countries).* Thus, while aggregate GDP at current prices for 1979 was 7.7 times its counterpart for 1970, that of the oil-exporting countries was 11.2 times, and that of the oil-producing countries 9.1 times. GDP per capita reflected the trend in GDP rise in general terms, but not quite fully. The discrepancy arose from the fact that population increase in the Gulf area and in Libya was larger than in the other countries in the region, owing to the substantial influx of expatriate manpower seeking employment in the oil-exporting countries, estimated at 3 million Arabs.

Substantial though the increase in GDP was in the seventies, it did not significantly alter the relative position of the Arab countries in the larger community of Third World countries, except, understandably, for the group of six Arab countries (Iraq, Kuwait, United Arab Emirates, Qatar, Saudi Arabia, and Libya) designated by the World Bank as 'capital-surplus oil exporters', according to a categorization based on GNP per capita. The remaining six oil producers (including Algeria, which is a member of OPEC) fall within the other GNP per capita categories. A word of explanation is called for here, as will become clear shortly.

Five Arab countries are omitted from the Bank's statistics in its 1980 *Report.* These are Djibouti, Bahrain, United Arab Emirates, Qatar, and Oman. The first can be left out, as it is

*The term 'oil-exporting countries' refers to the seven Arab members of OPEC, namely, Iraq, Kuwait, United Arab Emirates, Qatar, Saudi Arabia, Libya, and Algeria. To these must be added Bahrain, Oman, Syria, Egypt, and Tunisia, making the group of twelve 'oil-producing countries'.

also excluded from the Country Tables of AFESD, and the information available refers to 1974 or 1975. The remaining four are oil-producing countries, and two of them are OPEC members, and capital-surplus countries as well. Apart from the six Arab capital-surplus countries, there are fourteen countries that fit into the two average GNP categories of the World Bank: the low-income countries, and the medium-income countries. The first category had a weighted average GNP per capita of $200 for 1978; the second of $1,250. Two of the three Arab countries fitting into the first category had a GNP per capita in excess of the average. But the second category includes thirteen Arab countries (eleven already there, and two left out by the World Bank). Only three of the thirteen have a GNP per capita in excess of the average: Algeria (already in the World Bank tables), Bahrain, and Oman. The remaining ten countries all fall below the average. It is interesting also to note that none of the six non-Arab members of OPEC except Iran was a capital-surplus oil exporter in 1978, whereas all the Arab members except Algeria were capital-surplus countries. (Iran itself fell out of the list in 1979.)

There is a disturbing significance in these observations. This is that, apart from the export of oil, the majority of Arab economies have to their credit a performance, expressed in terms of GNP per capita, below that of their reference group in the Third World. Only in the category of low-income countries is the Arab showing slightly better, but this is little consolation, owing to the small advantage recorded there. Several of the non-Arab countries in the group of medium income with a GNP per capita above average are Latin American, but some are East Asian.

Obviously, the relative position of a country in a scale of GNP per capita depends on the GNP boundaries of the categories chosen, and therefore the position of the Arab medium-income countries would rise were the upper boundary to be lowered – that is, were the category to exclude some of the higher medium-income countries. On the other hand, the system of categorization is well defended in the World Bank's *World Development Report*, and it is useful to retain it for use as the basis for self-examination in order to discover why the Arab countries' economic performance is not better. This self-examination constitutes the subject-matter of the final chapter of the book. At this point it is necessary only to record that the performance could be distinctly better if the major development issues discussed in the final chapter were attended to in depth, with continuity, and within a regional Arab framework.

Another significant but disturbing observation relates to those Arab countries whose GDP per capita is very high – namely, the capital-surplus oil exporters. In their case the cause for concern is the extreme dependence on the oil sector, which accounts for a proportion of GDP ranging between 55.9 per cent for Libya and 83 per cent for Qatar, as Table 19 shows. Reference has been made to this dependence in an earlier chapter. Here we would add that the sector is one in which the large value added, or the contribution, of the sector to GDP is not a reflection of the inherent developmental and productive capability of the sector or of the society at large, but of the nature of oil as a strategic and most essential resource, and of the fact that this natural asset is exchanged in excessively large quantities for financial assets. The revenues include an inordinately large element of 'economic rent', or a surplus deriving from the special advantage enjoyed by the country which possesses the resource.

Earlier chapters of the book have dealt, among other things, with human and land resources, Arab oil and gas, and the region's efforts towards industrialization, and have tried to evaluate the achievements and identify the shortcomings in the performance of individual sectors and activities. The present chapter therefore attempts to provide a global appreciation of the performance of the economies of the region and, in so doing, indicate where the major failings lie. This will prepare the ground for a more specific examination in the final chapter of the basic development issues and tasks that have yet to be dealt with successfully. Essentially, the approach of this chapter will throughout be founded on the national accounts and what they tell us of the economic capability of the region and the structure of its economies.

Global performance can be evaluated from several angles. A number are used in the present survey. One is the performance with respect to production: the variety of goods and services produced, the quantity, and the quality of production. Obviously, in a short book we cannot undertake a detailed, specific examination of the three aspects of productive capability: diversification, volume, and quality. But, in general terms, it can be said that the process of diversification has intensified over the decades, more dramatically in the oil-exporting countries, considering the very narrow range of products which constitutes the base for comparison, but to a more limited extent in most of the non-oil countries. In all instances, the range of goods and services produced or capable of being produced in the near future, once the projects in the pipeline are completed, has increased considerably . but, more significantly, it now shows a greater complexity and sophistication. This greater differentiation contributes to the greater satisfaction of users' wants and needs, and the expanded productive capability suggests an increased technological capability.

The countries which are not oil exporters have been stimulated to diversify production and to increase its volume and improve its quality, in their desire to substitute for a larger array of imports, and to have a better chance to export. The oil-exporting countries have also wanted to consolidate their transition from the production of a few simple, conventional goods and services, to that of a much wider range of modern goods and services. But in addition they have been motivated by the desire to achieve a transition from the export of hydrocarbons in the crude form to more and more processed products of refining, and to petrochemical industries, along with the services associated with the hydrocarbon industry broadly defined. However, though the future promises much wider diversification in the oil-producing countries in general, and further diversification in the non-oil countries, the scope is vast for yet greater diversification and for improvement in the quality of goods and services produced, as well as for a drop in production costs and selling prices to make the products more competitive.

The overall concern of oil-exporting countries has been to accelerate their development, in order to have alternative sources of income to compensate for the decline in oil export

TABLE 18

Arab countries: sectoral contribution to GDP, 1970/9
(at factor cost and in million US dollars, at current prices)

Country/Year	Total GDP	Agriculture	Mining and Quarrying	Manufacturing (a)	Construction	Services
Iraq 1970 (b)	3,352.2	579.3	1,037.4	360.4	113.7	1,261.4
1979 (b)	30,709.5	1,737.1	19,871.9	1,875.3	1,167.6	6,057.6
Kuwait 1970	2,690.8	11.2	1,825.6	215.6	95.2	543.2
1979	23,293.0	52.9	16,844.1	1,361.6	579.5	4,454.9
Saudi Arabia 1970 (c)	3,811.7	218.7	1,811.8	432.3	207.5	1,141.4
1979 (c)	99,459.6	901.1	61,517.8	4,065.7	12,766.3	20,208.7
Bahrain 1970 (b)	244.2	2.1	183.8	6.1	4.2	48.0
1979 (b)	2,330.3	33.4	804.9	307.8	220.2	964.0
Qatar (d) 1970	302.0	3.0	211.0	8.0	—	80.0
1979	3,764.1	75.3	3,124.2	75.3	—	489.3
UAE 1970	1,470.4	37.8	934.6	59.3	93.0	345.7
1979	20,225.0	141.6	12,617.6	918.2	1,502.6	5,045.0
Oman 1970 (b)	256.1	39.8	171.8	0.7	25.4	18.4
1979 (b)	3,358.2	91.8	2,040.5	55.6	321.4	848.9
Yemen A.R. 1970 (b)	307.8	126.5	2.7	12.9	15.8	149.9
1979 (b)	2,660.3	1,068.0	29.0	152.0	249.3	1,162.0
P.D.R. Yemen 1970	167.3	31.6	0.1	43.6	1.6	90.4
1979	603.7	99.9	1.4	98.1	86.1	318.2
Jordan 1970	433.3	43.7	10.4	39.5	21.6	318.1
1979	1,802.9	149.7	91.5	269.5	143.1	1,149.1

Syria 1970 (e)	1,683.9	361.2	34.0	296.9	58.9	932.9
1979	9,388.4	1,862.7	943.3	992.1	644.4	4,945.9
Lebanon 1970 (f)	1,488.5	136.1	—	202.2	66.7	1,083.5
1979	2,523.0	215.2	76.1	391.0	86.3	1,754.4
Egypt 1970 (g)	6,212.3	1,780.2	121.9	1,375.4	278.3	2,656.5
1979	23,691.3	6,199.1	3,315.8	3,777.2	1,009.2	9,390.0
Sudan 1970 (b)	2,559.1	1,028.6	8.3	333.4	115.4	1,073.4
1979	4,786.2	1,981.1	15.3	527.6	218.5	2,043.7
Libya 1970 (b)	3,876.3	92.7	2,275.3	98.8	286.7	1,122.8
1979	22,246.9	563.8	12,431.0	798.2	2,555.6	5,898.3
Tunisia 1970	1,250.0	241.5	77.5	140.2	93.3	697.5
1979	5,922.0	993.1	556.7	841.5	509.4	3,021.3
Algeria 1970 (b)	4,827.0	615.8	798.7	813.4	504.9	2,094.2
1979	28,018.0	2,082.2	8,531.6	3,390.9	3,980.6	10,032.7
Morocco 1970 (e)	3,555.0	700.5	128.1	715.0	146.6	1,864.8
1979	14,664.1	2,653.1	683.4	2,896.6	1,153.0	7,278.0
Mauritania 1970 (b)	157.7	53.1	47.0	14.2	13.1	30.3
1979	550.7	172.7	72.0	59.7	41.3	205.0
Somalia 1970	189.2	70.4	12.3	13.6	8.7	84.2
1979	515.0	171.5	29.8	31.4	21.1	261.2
Djibouti 1970	104.0	5.0	—	6.0	9.0	84.0
1974	166.0	6.0	—	13.0	18.0	129.0
Total 1970	38,938.8	6,178.8	9,692.3	5,187.5	2,159.6	15,720.6
1979	300,678.2	21,251.3	143,597.9	22,898.3	27,273.5	85,657.2

Notes:
(a) Manufacturing includes electricity, gas, and water.
(b) Total GDP was computed from expenditure side and distributed among sectors according to 1977 structure.
(c) Value added in the mining sector was estimated from available data, while GDP in other sectors was estimated from expenditure

TABLE 18 (*cont.*)

side and distributed among non-oil sectors according to 1978 structure.

([d]) Total GDP for 1979 was obtained from source mentioned below and distributed among various sectors according to 1976 structure in UN sources.

([e]) Total GDP was computed from expenditure side and distributed among sectors according to 1978 structure.

([f]) No data available for 1979.

([g]) Provisional estimates.

([h]) Total GDP was computed from expenditure side and distributed among sectors according to 1976 structure.

Source: Arab Fund for Economic and Social Development, National Accounts Country Tables (Kuwait, 1980).

revenues, once these taper off. However, this transition is not yet reflected in the national accounts, particularly as presented in Table 19. There we see that the percentage contribution of every sector, except mining and (very moderately) construction, has declined between 1970 and 1979. But this merely reflects the vast and sudden expansion in the absolute contribution of the oil sector, well beyond any expansion registered in any other sector or, indeed, in the other sectors combined.

This can be clearly seen in Table 18, where the contribution of the sectors is given in money terms. With one exception, which deserves special explanation, in every oil-exporting country, more than half of the increase in GDP between 1970 and 1979 is accounted for by the oil sector alone. In Algeria, however, while this sector is the largest single contributor to the increase, its share in it is exactly one-third. The reason is the greater diversification that Algeria has succeeded in bringing about in the economy, where agriculture, manufacturing, construction, and services have all made substantial progress in absolute terms, though in relative terms it is only the mining (oil) sector that has made gains over the decade. Furthermore, the contribution of the oil sector to GDP, in relative terms, is the lowest among oil-exporting countries.

It is interesting also to note that the other five oil-producing countries (non-members of OPEC) show a markedly different pattern of economic diversification. Thus, three – Syria, Egypt, and Tunisia – show a very modest rise in the relative contribution of the oil sector, while the other two, Bahrain and Oman, show an actual drop. This indicates that the other sectors have in all five instances grown by wider strides than their counterparts in the oil-exporting countries. Yet this should not be taken to indicate greater diversification in the group of five countries; it merely means that the oil sector has not acquired the overwhelming preponderance that it has in the oil-exporting countries.

Irrespective of country or country grouping, the growth in productive capability (reflected in diversification, quantity, and quality) has been possible owing to the acquisition by Arab manpower of a wider variety and better quality of educational and technical skills, in addition to the satisfaction

TABLE 19

Arab countries: percentage sectoral contribution to GDP, 1970/9

Country/Year	Total GDP	Agriculture	Mining and Quarrying	Manufacturing	Construction	Services
Iraq 1970	100	17.3	30.9	10.8	3.4	37.6
1979	100	5.7	64.7	6.1	3.8	19.7
Kuwait 1970	100	0.5	67.8	8.0	3.5	20.2
1979	100	0.2	72.3	5.9	2.5	19.1
Saudi Arabia 1970	100	5.8	47.5	11.3	5.4	30.0
1979	100	0.9	61.9	4.1	12.8	20.3
Bahrain 1970	100	0.9	75.3	2.5	1.7	19.6
1979	100	1.4	34.5	13.2	9.5	41.4
Qatar 1970	100	1.0	69.9	2.6	—	26.5
1979	100	2.0	83.0	2.0	—	13.0
UAE 1970	100	2.6	63.6	4.0	6.3	23.5
1979	100	0.7	62.4	4.5	7.4	25.0
Oman 1970	100	15.5	67.0	0.3	10.0	7.2
1979	100	2.7	60.8	1.7	9.5	25.3
Yemen A.R. 1970	100	41.1	0.9	4.2	5.1	48.7
1979	100	40.1	1.1	5.7	9.4	43.7
P.D.R. Yemen 1970	100	18.9	0.1	26.0	1.0	54.0
1979	100	16.5	0.2	16.3	14.3	52.7
Jordan 1970	100	10.1	2.4	9.1	5.0	73.4
1979	100	8.3	5.2	14.9	7.9	63.7
Syria 1970	100	21.5	2.0	17.6	3.5	55.4
1979	100	19.8	10.0	10.6	6.9	52.7

Lebanon 1970	100	9.1	—	13.6	4.5	72.8
1979	100	8.5	3.0	15.5	3.5	69.5
Egypt 1970	100	28.7	2.0	22.1	4.5	42.7
1979	100	26.2	14.0	15.9	4.3	39.6
Sudan 1970	100	40.2	0.4	13.0	4.5	41.9
1979	100	41.4	0.3	11.0	4.6	42.7
Libya 1970	100	2.4	58.7	2.5	7.4	29.0
1979	100	2.5	55.9	3.6	11.5	26.5
Tunisia 1970	100	19.3	6.2	11.2	7.5	55.8
1979	100	16.8	9.4	14.2	8.6	51.0
Algeria 1970	100	12.8	16.5	16.9	10.5	43.3
1979	100	7.4	30.5	12.1	14.2	35.8
Morocco 1970	100	19.7	3.6	20.1	4.1	52.5
1979	100	18.0	4.7	19.8	7.9	49.6
Mauritania 1970	100	33.7	29.8	9.0	8.3	19.2
1979	100	31.4	31.1	10.8	7.5	37.2
Somalia 1970	100	37.2	6.5	7.2	4.6	44.5
1979	100	33.3	5.8	6.1	4.1	50.7
Djibouti 1970	100	4.8	—	5.8	8.7	80.7
1979	100	3.7	—	7.8	10.8	77.7
Total 1970	100	15.9	24.9	13.3	5.5	40.4
1979	100	7.1	47.8	7.6	9.1	28.4

Source: Table 18.

of various other conditions necessary to development.* Although earlier chapters incorporated some criticism of education in the Arab region, and of the process of the acquisition and adaptation of technological capability, this is only one part of the record. The other part reflects marked advances, compared with the conditions prevailing in the 1930s.

In fact, the criticism levelled at the performance in the fields of education and technical training derives essentially from a sensation of awe in face of the enormity of the development tasks ahead, and the feeling that much more yet could have been achieved, particularly after the acquisition of political independence and, especially, since the early seventies. Nevertheless, the record of the region in education and technical training is on the whole good, although it is not as creditable as that of Latin America or South and South-east Asia – at least, at the primary and secondary levels of education.[63] The overall generalization that can be made in respect of health-related indicators in the Arab region compared with other regions (availability of physicians and nursing persons, access to safe water, daily calorie supply) is that the Arab position ranges between average and below-average, with few exceptions.[64]

Two important sectors which have received attention (and some sizeable investment allocations) over the decades, especially since independence, and which constitute one important aspect of economic performance are construction and transport and communication. Neither has been discussed in earlier chapters, and this is added reason for reference to them here, even if brief. Both are necessary as supplementary sectors serving activities in agriculture, manufacturing, trade, and banking. But construction is also important in itself, inasmuch as all structures constitute one form or another of construction and, moreover, housing consists basically of construction activity, and housing is of social as well as economic significance. It is interesting to note that construction

*These include the emergence of national states when colonialism receded, institution-building, the rising expectations and expanded demands of the masses, expanded employment in the absolute, and increased and diversified investment. The last two factors will be dealt with later in the chapter.

has always received relatively large investment allocations, from the private as well as the public sector. On the other hand, the transport and communication sector has had a larger component of public sector investment put into it, owing to the public nature of roads, railways, ports, telecommunications, and the airways in virtually all the countries in the region.

Table 23, which we shall discuss later, shows the importance attached to construction and to transport and communication, as reflected in investment allocations in development plans. There is physical witness to these allocations, in the housing and public building projects; in factory and office buildings; in construction on farms and plantations; in roads, railways, ports, airports, and airways; and in telephones and other telecommunication systems and facilities. Yet much more is still needed. As far as construction is concerned, the greatest need is low-income and middle-income housing. In transport and communication, there is a great need for public transport systems, railways, roads, bridges, and ports, but the most glaring need is for a regional approach to transport and communication. Much closer regional co-operation and complementarity in the provision of transport and communication systems and facilities is called for.

This need will be felt more strongly, the bigger the productive capacity, and the greater the volume of production and of trade both within and between countries. The shortcomings of the agricultural and manufacturing sectors, to which reference was made earlier, will demand urgent attention. But once the production of agricultural produce and manufactured goods increases, and distribution pressures rise, the acute need for transport and communication facilities will be apparent. The need for silos and other storage facilities and capacity, the supply of which is short even by present standards of production, will also become increasingly apparent. Performance is well below the acceptable minimum in this area of distribution, particularly if the matter of food security is borne in mind, and is to receive adequate attention.

A very important consideration in any evaluation of national economic performance is the employment which economic activity generates. Employment-generation is a

TABLE 20

Arab countries: percentage contribution of each country to total GDP by sectors, 1970/9

Country/Year	Total GDP	Agriculture	Mining and Quarrying	Manufacturing	Construction	Services
Iraq 1970	8.6	9.4	10.7	6.9	5.3	8.0
1979	10.2	8.2	13.8	8.2	4.3	7.1
Kuwait 1970	6.9	0.2	18.8	4.2	4.4	3.5
1979	7.7	0.2	11.7	5.9	2.1	5.2
Saudi Arabia 1970	9.8	3.5	18.7	8.3	9.6	7.3
1979	33.1	4.2	42.8	17.8	46.8	23.6
Bahrain 1970	0.6	0.0	1.9	0.1	0.2	0.3
1979	0.8	0.2	0.6	1.3	0.8	1.1
Qatar 1970	0.8	0.0	2.2	0.2	—	0.5
1979	1.3	0.4	2.2	0.3	—	0.6
UAE 1970	3.8	0.6	9.6	1.4	4.3	2.2
1979	6.7	0.7	8.8	4.0	5.5	5.9
Oman 1970	0.7	0.6	1.8	—	1.2	0.1
1979	1.1	0.4	1.4	0.2	1.2	1.0
Yemen A.R. 1970	0.8	2.0	0.0	0.2	0.7	1.0
1979	0.9	5.0	0.0	0.7	0.9	1.4
P.D.R. Yemen 1970	0.4	0.5	0.0	0.8	0.1	0.6
1979	0.2	0.5	0.0	0.4	0.3	0.4
Jordan 1970	1.1	0.7	0.1	0.8	1.0	2.0
1979	0.6	0.7	0.1	1.2	0.5	1.3
Syria 1970	4.3	5.8	0.4	5.7	2.7	5.9
1979	3.1	8.8	0.7	4.3	2.4	5.8

Lebanon 1970	3.8	2.2	—	3.9	3.1	6.9
1979	0.8	1.0	0.1	1.7	0.3	2.0
Egypt 1970	15.9	28.8	1.3	26.5	12.9	16.9
1979	7.9	29.2	2.3	16.5	3.7	11.0
Sudan 1970	6.6	16.6	0.1	6.4	5.3	6.8
1979	1.6	9.3	0.0	2.3	0.8	2.4
Libya 1970	9.9	1.5	23.4	1.9	13.3	7.1
1979	7.4	2.7	8.7	3.5	9.4	6.9
Tunisia 1970	3.2	3.9	0.8	2.7	4.3	4.4
1979	2.0	4.8	0.4	3.7	1.9	3.5
Algeria 1970	12.4	10.0	8.2	15.7	23.4	13.3
1979	9.3	9.8	5.9	14.8	14.6	11.7
Morocco 1970	9.1	11.3	1.3	13.8	6.8	11.9
1979	4.9	12.5	0.5	12.6	4.2	8.5
Mauritania 1970	0.4	0.9	0.5	0.3	0.6	0.2
1979	0.2	0.8	0.1	0.3	0.2	0.2
Somalia 1970	0.5	1.1	0.1	0.2	0.4	0.5
1979	0.2	0.8	0.0	0.1	0.1	0.3
Djibouti 1970	0.3	0.1	—	0.1	0.4	0.5
1979	0.1	0.8	—	0.1	0.1	0.2
Total 1970	100	100	100	100	100	100
1979	100	100	100	100	100	100

Note: Totals do not add to 100 because of rounding.

Source: Table 18.

crucial test of successful development on the level of the entire economy, that is, disregarding pockets of unemployment that might appear here and there as a result of modernization, or because of competition between closely-related or substitutable activities or products. But the economy as a whole cannot be said to be developing healthily if its total activity results in the global reduction of both employment opportunities and actual employment. This assertion is based on obvious social grounds as much as on purely economic grounds. In the latter context, increased unemployment means reduced income for the unemployed, and therefore shrunken purchasing power.

Development in the Arab region has not been particularly successful in providing increased employment opportunities parallel with increased investment and national product. This has happened although the total labour supply itself is somewhat restricted by the large proportion of dependants among Arab populations, at the lower end of the age scale. (This is due to the high rate of natural increase of population which results in 55 per cent of the population being under 20 years of age.) In addition, the number of those qualified to join the gainfully active population is further reduced because of the low levels of education and training prevailing in general, and the low participation of women in the labour force.

The energetic drive for economic development occurs in a contradictory situation: a large reservoir of unemployed men and women alongside shortages in manpower not only within specific countries but also at the regional level. The explanation is that the unemployed are largely incapable of finding jobs, because they are short of skills and/or a minimum level of functional literacy; and the areas of shortage relate to skills not in sufficient supply. Hence the movement across national frontiers within the Arab region of some 3 million Arabs in search of employment, and, in addition, the presence of hundreds of thousands of non-Arab expatriate labourers in the oil-producing countries in the Gulf area.

Employment statistics are of low reliability in the region, particularly those of partial employment. Nevertheless, according to Table 21, which provides an order of magnitude with respect to the volume of employment, the total active population is about one-fourth of total population. This is a low proportion, but it is explainable in view of, among other things, the high rate of dependency already mentioned. Just over half of the total active population is engaged in agricultural and related primary activities, while some 19 per cent are engaged in industry (broadly defined to include manufacturing, electricity, gas, and water, as well as construction), and the balance of 30 per cent are employed in the various service sectors.

The high absorption in agriculture is deceptive, since it conceals a large proportion of underemployment or disguised unemployment, owing to the seasonality of agricultural activity. Thus, in fact, actual full employment (or its equivalent, if conversion were made from seasonal to full employment at the coefficients normally used for the purpose) would be lower than the 25 per cent to which reference was made in the last paragraph – other things being equal. In brief, account must be taken of the discrepancy between the potentially active population, that is, those between 15 and 64 years of age of both sexes, who according to the World Bank constituted between 50 and 54 per cent of total population for 1978 (or some 80 million Arabs), and these actually in active employment (39 million as in Table 21). But even if we excluded secondary school and university students who are over 15 years of age (totalling over 6.5 million) and members of the armed forces – categories that do not feature in employment statistics – we would still be left with a labour supply in excess of 72 million. The volume of actual employment would thus be found to hover around 55 per cent of the potential supply of labour. The very large gap this constitutes would be wider still if account were also to be taken of under-employment.

This conclusion may, however, be qualified. The underutilization of around 33 million men and women is basically explainable in terms of the very low recorded female participation in the labour force; the highest rate is thought to be in Lebanon where female participation accounts for about 15 per cent of the active labour force. In most other countries the rate is considerably lower. On the other side, there is a

TABLE 21

Arab countries: employment by sectors, 1977
(thousands)

Country	Total active population	Employment in: Agriculture	Industry ([a])	Construction	Services
Iraq	3,028	1,710	306	(79)	1,012
Kuwait	317	9	67	(32)	241
Saudi Arabia	1,994	631	344	(209)	1,019
Bahrain	68	4	21	(14)	43
Qatar	89	3	25	(–)	61
UAE	487	12	231	(175)	244
Oman ([b])	214	136	–	–	78 ([c])
Yemen A.R.	1,150	888	50	(23)	212
P.D.R. Yemen	371	182	38	(17)	151
Jordan	653	189	174	(85)	290
Syria	1,830	878	358	(126)	594
Lebanon ([b])	793	103	214	–	476
Egypt ([b])	10,427	5,318	2,711	–	2,398
Sudan ([b])	5,065	4,001	507	–	557
Libya ([b])	650	143	176	–	331
Tunisia ([b])	1,446	622	333	–	491
Algeria ([b])	3,744	1,310	674	–	1,760
Morocco ([b])	4,872	2,582	926	–	1,364
Mauritania ([b])	461	387	23	–	51
Somalia ([b])	1,310	1,087	92	–	131
Total	38,969	20,195	7,270		11,504
Per cent of total		51.8	18.7		29.5

Notes

(*a*) Including mining, manufacturing, electricity, gas and water, and construction.
(*b*) See source 2 below.
(*c*) Including industry since no further breakdown is given in the source.

Sources: (1) ECWA, *Statistical Abstract of the Region of the Economic Commission for Western Asia*, 1980, for countries of ECWA Region except Lebanon, Oman, and Egypt. (2) United Nations Conference on Trade and Development, *Handbook of International Trade and Development Statistics, 1979* for total active population of countries marked (*b*), and World Bank, *World Development Report, 1979* for the breakdown of employment.

balancing factor: the oversight or non-inclusion of millions of women who are actively engaged, though not at full capacity, in agricultural and pastoral activities. In fairness, to these must be added women doing unpaid housework, full time or part time, whose labour has indeed an economic value to the extent that it has an opportunity cost. Together, the two groups of women would absorb a good part of the 33 million gap to which we have just referred. However, on balance and as far as recorded employment or employment as usually estimated goes, there is a large volume of involuntary unemployment made up of some 15 million men and women whom the development process has still failed to absorb into gainful and productive employment.

Comparisons cannot be made with the early thirties with respect to employment. This is primarily because data were then available for a very few countries only, namely Egypt, Palestine, and, on an even smaller scale, the Maghreb countries. Moreover, those data were at best very rough estimates. Any attempt at comparison would therefore prove fruitless.

Investment, which is a major factor in new job creation (along with the improvement of the qualifications of manpower for work), has risen in both absolute and relative terms over the past decade. If the thirty-year stretch 1945–74 is considered on its own, investment will be found to have been roughly 15 per cent of GDP, averaged both for countries and for years. The proportion has risen markedly since 1974, to reach 29 per cent in 1979 (see Table 22). If the steep rise in GDP is remembered, it will be seen that the rise in investment in absolute terms is indeed considerable, even allowing for inflation in the seventies. A comparison between 1970 and 1979 is very revealing: gross investment in the former year was $7.5 billion, while it stood at $87.5 billion for the latter year.[65] Even if we deflate the latter figure by a factor of 3 for inflation, the result would still indicate that investment in 1979 was about four times its counterpart in 1974.

An increasing part of this investment has been made by the government (including the public sector) over the independence era. Today public investment is considerably over half total investment, and much of it submits to or is guided by development plans. These plans have different levels of

TABLE 22

Gross investment in the Arab countries, 1979
(million US dollars)

Country	Investment
Iraq	11,174.5
Kuwait	2,680.4
Saudi Arabia	26,084.0
Bahrain	402.9
Qatar	794.9
UAE	6,157.9
Oman	903.9
Yemen A.R.	990.3
P.D.R. Yemen	194.3
Jordan	815.1
Syria	3,033.0
Lebanon (1977)	833.3
Egypt	6,054.9
Sudan	694.9
Libya	6,041.5
Tunisia	2,096.5
Algeria	14,740.6
Morocco	3,368.7
Mauritania	266.3
Somalia	178.3
Total	87,506.2

Source: AFESD, National Account Country Tables.

sophistication and coverage, and also of authority or mandate. On the whole, the expanding and strengthened role of the government and the growing importance of planning (as a concept and a policy tool) are undeniable realities. Even countries considering themselves staunch supporters of private enterprise have large development plans, and channel most of their investment via the government. This trend has three significant implications.

The first relates to both the impact of investment that is channelled according to central plans on the pattern of allocation and to the effect of these resources. Table 23 shows the large volume of investment allocations in the development plans of the countries covered, in the period 1974–81, mostly in the form of 5-year plans and mostly for the years 1976–80. The total allocations amount to $326

TABLE 23

Arab countries (a): investment allocations according to development plans in the second half of the seventies (million US dollars)

Country	Plan period	Total investment	Average annual investment	Percentage of investment in sectors (b) Agriculture	Industry and mining	Construction	Transport and communication	Other sectors
Iraq	76–80	45,561 (c)	9112	23.6	24.2	17.4	17.4	17.4
Kuwait	76–80	16,609	3322	0.7	20.5	30.8	16.0	32.1
Saudi Arabia	75–80	140,346	23391	0.9	9.0	14.6	8.1	67.3
UAE	77–79	4,385	1462	n.a.	n.a.	n.a.	n.a.	n.a.
Oman	76–80	3,922	784	n.a.	n.a.	n.a.	n.a.	n.a.
Yemen A.R.	76–80	3,500 (c)	700	14.2	22.2	2.8	30.8	29.9
P.D.R. Yemen	74–79	216	43	35.0	10.0	—	25.0	30.0
Jordan	76–80	2,308	464	5.2	30.1	11.1	19.0	34.6
Syria	76–80	13,712 (c)	2742	23.9	20.8	14.9	10.4	29.9
Lebanon	72–77	539	90	n.a.	n.a.	n.a.	n.a.	n.a.
Egypt	76–80	20,407	4081	3.5	22.1	16.0	31.1	27.3
Sudan	77–83	6,030	1005	22.6	28.6	—	23.7	25.0
Libya	76–80	24,219	4844	17.6	15.4	11.2	14.2	41.5
Tunisia	77–81	9,790 (c)	1958	11.9	47.3	1.2	13.6	26.0
Algeria	74–77	27,575	6894	11.0	24.5	8.8	9.6	46.1
Morocco	73–77	6,179	1236	16.3	5.4	2.7	13.9	61.7
Mauritania	76–80	206 (c)	41	n.a.	n.a.	n.a.	n.a.	n.a.
Somalia	74–78	615	123	36.6	16.4	4.0	24.5	18.5
Total		326,119						

Notes

([a]) No plans included for Bahrain, Qatar, and Djibouti.

([b]) The percentage distribution of investment relates to the plans as originally published, before later amendments were introduced.

([c]) Conversion of national currencies into US dollars effected at 1977 rates of exchange.

Sources AFESD, *Study on the Development of Human and Manpower Resources in the Arab Region* (Kuwait, March 1978; in Arabic); pp. 17, 43, 44.

billion, or \$65 billion annually on average. The growth they are capable of bringing about is, again on average, some 7 per cent per annum.

This expectation of growth is, however, qualified by two factors: first, only some 70 per cent of the allocations actually materialize, and not all investments made by the private sector are included in the plan projections. Furthermore, the allocations generally rise as the years go by, and the average does not provide a correct estimate of the allocations for the terminal year. The second qualification is that actual growth is considerably influenced by oil exports and revenue, which are largely unrelated to any one year's investments – or to new investment at all, for that matter – in the sense that the existing oil production facilities permit expansion in production with only very modest variable costs, and oil prices are an autonomous factor (that is, determined by the government concerned). These qualifications operate in different directions, which makes it very difficult, if not impossible, to estimate the subsequent increase in GDP on the basis of economic factors alone.

The second implication of the pattern of investment concerns the sectoral structure of the economy, inasmuch as the distribution of investment by sector influences the distribution of value added, that is, the relative contribution of the various sectors to GDP. The influence is not felt immediately, owing to the accumulated influence of past investments, but it is real none the less. Table 19 provided a picture of the pattern of relative significance, in terms of their contribution, of the various sectors. Table 20, on the other hand, showed the country-by-country contribution to the value added in each sector. We are here more concerned with Table 19. Two observations regarding structure are relevant at this point. The first is essentially descriptive. It is that the relative sectoral contributions vary widely, both from country to country and from decade to decade. Although Table 19 provides information for one decade only, information is available for about thirty years beginning with the early fifties, and it confirms the finding that there is considerable structural transformation over time, as well as differentiation between countries. The pattern of transformation is not uniform either way, but it has certain marked aspects. One of these is the relative decline of agriculture; a second is the steep rise of the hydrocarbon sector, particularly in the oil-exporting countries, but also in the other oil-producing countries. A third is the very large 'contribution' of the service sectors, a feature to which we shall turn in the second observation, which follows. A fourth is the sluggishness of manufacturing industry, contrary to expectations (see Chapter 3 above). The second observation can probably be regarded as normative, or value-loaded in part. It concerns the change in the structure in recent years, particularly the social and economic dangers inherent in the heavy dependence on the oil sector (that is, inherent in its very large contribution).

A new pattern has arisen over the seventies, one characterized by a large cluster of service sectors, some of which do not reflect a rise in production or productivity in any meaningful sense. We refer here to the expansion in foreign trade and internal commerce that is dependent on the increased consumption of luxury goods and services, mainly through imitation or the demonstration effect, without such consumption leading to a lasting satisfaction of genuine needs. Indeed, many of the wants thus satisfied are artificially created by promotion and advertising campaigns, initiated by large enterprises usually associated with transnational corporations. Again, through the same mechanism, the wants are transformed into imagined needs.[66] In this category may be included the services of middlemen and intermediaries, speculators, in addition to excessively luxurious hotels and pleasure spots, and the like. But, above all, we would single out the growing dependence of the newly-rich on their 'earnings' in the form of interest and dividends which accrue without commensurate effort. This phenomenon is known in the economic literature as 'unearned income', and its increasing magnitude is turning a large part of Arab society into a *rentier* society. The deleterious effect of this disparity between effort and reward on Arab society can hardly be exaggerated.[67]

Finally, the third implication of the increased investment effected via the government and the public sector concerns the prevailing socio-economic system. It has been indicated that the government has acquired a vastly augmented role in virtually all Arab countries, even in those that are staunch supporters of free enterprise and the market mechanism. These same countries now formulate central development plans and publicize them. It is true that the plans are often no more than listings of projects strung together, or broad programmes rather than full plans. It is also true that even the full plans are not always comprehensive: they do not contain the investment allocations mandatory in the public sector or the outline plans that are really intended as possible guidelines for private-sector investments. Nevertheless, not only has planning become acceptable in all countries but fashionable as well. This in itself reflects a basic change of attitude. Behind this change lies the realization that as applied in the Arab region, the private enterprise system and the centrally-planned system can be linked or reconciled, and, indeed, are not very far apart.

The linkage is effected at two points. The adoption of widening welfare systems operated by government in several Arab countries is one such point. The other is the selective acceptance of a centrally-planned system in which the private sector retains a respectable area of action. The selectivity is based on the retention of the profit motive and its continued respect and application as a criterion of performance. Indeed, of nowhere in the Arab world can it be said that the philosophical tenets of socialism and the strategies, policies, and mechanisms that translate it into fact have become the basis for the life of its society or for the operation of its economy.

9. Regional economic co-operation and complementarity

Regional co-operation is the minimum state of interaction and mutual help among the Arab countries which the Arab nationalists desire to see. Ideally, what is hoped for is a higher state of cohesiveness which grows firmer, more effective, and more comprehensive, through the higher states of complementarity and integration, until it reaches one of organic unity. Moreover, this ideal is not restricted to the economic sphere but embraces also the cultural, strategic, and political. The ideal and the desire are not inspired merely by the cultural ties that bind the region's countries together, nor by its shared experiences and history, nor yet by the Arabs' hopes and expectations for the future, although all these are strong operative factors. Co-operation, complementarity or integration, and unity can also be justified by hard economic necessity and purely economic considerations.

The fact that a higher form of co-operation, such as strong complementarity and integration, has not yet fully emerged is the result of the weakness of neither non-economic nor economic justification: rather it is the result of foreign interference with the hopes of the masses interacting with certain partial vested interests. These are variously motivated by narrow economic, political, or separatist racial or other minority considerations.

It is intended in the present chapter to trace briefly the history of intraregional economic relations and co-operation, and to identify the areas of co-operation that have received emphasis and the avenues that have been pursued with a view to intensifying the co-operation and bringing about a state of close economic complementarity – in the sense of translating potential complementarity into actual complementarity. In the process, certain major mechanisms or institutions created for the purpose will be identified and discussed. Finally, the state of co-operation now prevailing – and here we use the word 'co-operation' in a broad sense to describe all forms of regional economic cohesiveness that have developed, leaving more specific characterization till later – will be reported, and the progress achieved will be assessed. The present discussion contains a certain amount of critical analysis, but a fuller examination of the issues and tasks of regional co-operation will be undertaken in Chapter 11, which will be concerned also with the future of regional economic co-operation as a major factor in Arab economic development.

Economic relations between the Arab countries are of long standing, dating back to the days of the vast Arab empire, and those of the Ottoman empire. In modern times, relations between parts of the Fertile Crescent, or between Lebanon, Syria, and Palestine on the one hand, and Egypt on the other, have again been strong since the First World War. 'The oldest instances of co-operation in modern times formalised in trade agreements can be encountered in the pre-independence era. These were between Syria and Lebanon . . . , between Syria and Palestine, Transjordan and Syria, Transjordan and Palestine, Transjordan and Hejaz (part of today's Saudi Arabia), Egypt and Syria, and Egypt and Palestine – all in the 1920's',[68] and all in the Mashreq. The Maghreb countries under French colonial rule also had formalized trade arrangements among themselves and between them and France. In the Mashreq, all but the Syro-Lebanese customs union were disrupted and discontinued in the years preceding the Second World War. The union itself was broken in 1950. It is useful here to quote at some length from a study of Arab economic development.

> The only case of multilateral cooperation preceding the formation of the League of Arab States was the Middle East Supply Center, set up in 1940 by Great Britain, to be joined two years later by the United States. The MESC included 18 political entities, 6 of which were non-Arab . . . Its objectives were to assure and regulate the imports of essential commodities to the region, to provide the necessary shipping in stringent wartime conditions, and to promote local production and intraregional exchanges and thus reduce the need for imports. To achieve these ends, the MESC developed planning, control, guidance and assistance functions and mechanisms in its headquarters in Cairo and in its branch offices in the region. What is worth noting in this

connection and with respect to the bilateral trade agreements referred to before is that all these instances of cooperation materialised under the aegis of a foreign power which imposed its will. The lesson to be derived is not that Arab economic cooperation cannot proceed far without foreign domination, but that cooperation cannot be honestly pursued and materialise without the political will to bring it about at the highest decision-making level.

As an overall assessment, it can be said that cooperation represents the mainstream of Arab thinking and feeling. Evidence of this . . . comes from the fact that, as early as 1944 and 1945 when the Protocol forming the League of Arab States, and then its Charter, were drawn up and signed, it was stipulated that the League would undertake to bring about economic cooperation and organise it among the member states, and between these as a group and the group of non-members. Subsequent major documents, beginning with the Treaty for Joint Defence and Economic Cooperation, included clauses specifically stressing the pursuit of such cooperation. One of these clauses was of particular significance, as it stipulated for the formation of the Arab Economic Council which . . . was to suggest the ways and means for economic development, cooperation, and organization and coordination.

The Economic Council was not particularly active or effective. In 1957 it drew up an agreement for Arab economic unity, but there was no authority capable of implementing this agreement until, in 1962, the Council for Arab Economic Unity was formed. Two more years were to pass before the Council had enough members to approve and ratify the agreement and make it binding. The same year, 1964, witnessed the setting-up of the Arab Common Market as a first step towards economic unity.

Between 1953 (when the first major economic agreement was signed) and November 1980, when the Council of Arab Heads of State (the Summit) signed an agreement for the guarantee of Arab investments within the region, many agreements were entered into: some – like the economic unity agreement of 1957 and the common market agreement of 1964 – achieved only limited support. In addition, many institutions and mechanisms were established to serve various purposes falling within the generic term of 'economic co-operation'.[69] These come under several categories: some are official organizations (specialized agencies) formed within the framework of the Arab League, such as the Arab League Educational, Cultural, and Scientific Organization, the Arab Organization for Industrial Development, and two dozen other organizations; some are autonomous bodies, such as the Organization of Arab Petroleum Exporting Countries, the Arab Fund for Economic and Social Development, and the Arab Monetary Fund; some are Arab professional (syndical) unions, such as the federations of Arab economists, bankers, labourers, engineers, and so on; some are production and service companies (potash, tankers, re-insurance, marine transport, fishing); some are groupings or unions of industries in the fields of iron and steel, textiles, chemical products, and insurance. In all they number several dozen institutions, and their capital by the end of 1980 was in excess of $23 billion. In addition, there are joint ventures between two or more countries in the fields of banking, real estate, and industry.

Economic relations and interactions among institutions and individuals in the private sector have also become substantial. They take several forms and consist of business associations in the fields of finance, trade, tourism, industry, and real estate, as well as travel and employment. Their significance in promoting cohesion and integration is enormous and must not be underestimated.

Thus, it can be said that a relatively large 'joint Arab economic sector' (JAES) has developed over the years, whose work affects several spheres. Those falling within the domain of the Arab League or associated with it are:

Functional organizations or groupings, like the category referred to above.

Joint financing, comprising AFESD, AMF, and the Arab Authority for Agricultural Investment and Development. To this category must be added the national (country) institutions whose work covers the whole Arab region. Here we refer to the national development funds of Kuwait, Abu Dhabi, Saudi Arabia, and Iraq (aggregate capital $14 billion); the five companies established by the Organization of Arab Petroleum Exporting Countries for exploration, tankerage, and other services (aggregate capital about $3 billion); and government-to-government financial flows which do not go through the national funds. In all, the aid flows average some $5 billion a year.

The establishment of a few Arab training institutions at the regional level. Some of these are already in existence, while a few others are at the planning or execution stage. They include training in maritime affairs, planning, statistics, vocational training, and training in skills related to the oil sector (under the aegis of the Organization of Arab Petroleum Exporting Countries).

Finally, the many ministerial and other councils organized on a functional basis, which meet at regular intervals and constitute an important institutional mechanism of control, advisory, and co-ordinative service. The ministerial councils fall under two broad categories: groupings of specialized ministers (such as those of labour, finance, industry, agriculture, health, and the like) who hold meetings independently; and specialized ministers meeting in their capacity as governing councils of certain regional organizations, for example the ministers of industry meeting for business related to the Organization for Industrial Development, or the ministers of agriculture meeting as the governing council of the Organization for Agricultural Development, and the ministers of finance meeting as the governing council of the AFESD or AMF, and so on. It should be added that the council with the highest authority with respect to economic affairs is the Economic and Social Council, under whose jurisdiction are the various economic organizations and specialized bodies within the Arab League family. There is also the Council for Arab Economic Unity whose concern is essentially with the agreement of Arab economic unity and the agreement of the Arab Common Market, though its activity also reaches into some areas in which the Economic and Social Council is directly involved.

It would be misleading to trace the history of Arab co-operation without first indicating that the efforts deployed have on the whole involved, and drawn in, the countries of the Mashreq, as the Maghreb countries have, by and large, kept out of the organizations and agreements formed or entered into. The Maghreb countries have also attempted to draw closer together in the economic field, and to that end have formed a number of institutions and entered into certain agreements purporting to bring about closer economic co-operation and co-ordination among their members. These fall under the Maghreb Consultative Committee, headed by the Conference of Ministers of Economy, with a Permanent Committee and a Secretariat.* The two groups (the Mashreq and the Maghreb countries) have not linked their institutions and agreements together. But recently, with the inaction of Maghreb institutions and the non-implementation of the agreements entered into there, the Maghreb has drawn closer to the body of institutions and agreements of the Arab League and has joined most of these. Consequently, it can be said that the slow process, beginning with the Alexandria Protocol of 1944, has led up to the Arab Summit of November 1980, which was mainly concerned with economic issues, and which marked a new all-Arab vision or concept of Arab economic relations for the future, based on the cumulative experience of the past thirty-five years.

The JAES, which has taken shape over the years, though its progress was much more marked in the seventies, has been found to be unsatisfactory on several counts. This is not the place for a detailed evaluation of the JAES prior to 1980, it will be sufficient at this point to list its main shortcomings, and the major expectations from it. These are:

While it is true that the JAES now possesses a large body of institutions and agreements, these did not until 1980 submit to a disciplined system of priorities within the framework of an overall strategy for joint Arab economic action (SJAEA). Such a strategy was drawn up and approved by the Arab Economic Council in 1979, and by the Arab Summit in 1980. The future will determine and witness its impact on joint Arab economic action.

*Initially, Morocco, Algeria, Tunisia, and Libya were members of the Permanent Consultative Committee. But Libya withdrew from membership in 1970, while Mauritania became a member in 1975.

(The SJAEA was supplemented by thirty economic studies centring on three main themes of crucial significance to the development and security of the Arab nation. These studies are all programme- and action-oriented.)[70]

The SJAEA embodies a formula acceptable to all Arab governments; it is neither as weak and vague as mere 'co-operation', nor so strong or extreme as 'unity', which would arouse anxiety in certain Arab quarters. While the notion of the JAES may be a source of consolation and a factor for consensus, it could also dilute the desire for unity, or at least for complementarity and integration.

The SJAEA and the thirty studies supporting it are designed to go beyond the shortcomings of the JAES as it now stands. These are:

Although the organizations and agreements felt to be necessary for joint Arab economic action are already formed or entered into, much of the activity of the JAES is currently largely haphazard. Examples are the large movements of Arab labour across national frontiers, and the movement of capital from the oil-exporting to the capital-short countries. Commendable as these movements are, they are suboptimal in effect, because they do not submit to a plan or a system of priorities within an overall strategy formulated to serve the twin objectives of Arab development and Arab security.

Until very recently, much of the concern with economic complementarity has centred on the liberalization of trade within the region and the expansion of its volume. The new SJAEA, however, starts from the position that, first, there ought to be more production to enable the volume of trade to expand. Hence the emphasis on production within the content of complementarity. Secondly, this emphasis, along with that mentioned in the preceding paragraph, on a *planned* approach to complementarity, adds new dimensions to the objective by changing it from one with expansion of trade as its focal point to one which is both planned and productive.

Until very recently, the concept of joint projects or companies was restricted to joint financing. Complementarity must go well beyond that to involve the meshing or linkage of productive capacity in the Arab countries; this would involve vertical and/or horizontal integration, and would constitute a big step beyond mere joint financing.

These and other ideas are incorported in the SJAEA and in the studies prepared around it. Furthermore, joint Arab economic action is designed to operate within a plan for the JAES, according to a system of priorities. This system gives precedence to efforts and investments in the following sectors or areas of activity: manpower training and education; the acquisition of technological capability; food security; basic (engineering) industry; and energy. The financial sector is also a priority area, in that it has to be adjusted and restructured so as to serve the priorities adequately. And the whole priority system is designed to serve the objective of National (that is, regional) development, and National security. These objectives are believed to interact and to support and supplement each other. Similarly, country and regional action are believed to supplement and support each other. The whole system is so understood and designed as to assure complementarity rather than contradiction between the two pairs: development and security, and country and regional action.

If an overall evaluation is to be made here, it is first, that a great deal has been achieved in the realm of Arab economic co-operation and co-ordination, but that much more has yet to be done if the results are to be concrete and substantial, and if a worthwhile state of complementarity and integration is to be attained. Secondly, the performance aimed at for the future must be planned according to clearly defined priorities in order to achieve clearly defined objectives. Thirdly, this would require the deployment of substantially more financial resources on a regional basis than has been the case so far. Fourthly, joint Arab economic action, in the context of the

SJAEA, calls for close co-ordination among the Arab governments, as well as mutual accommodation of and adjustment in economic strategies, plans, and policies if effective complementarity is to be achieved. Consequently, the notion of the sovereignty of the Arab states should not be used as an excuse to evade such co-ordination and accommodation. But, finally, above all, there must be the political will to intensify and solidify joint Arab economic action and its institutions and programmes – a will born of the conviction that joint Arab economic action can serve both development and security, at country and at regional levels, and that these objectives are worth all the effort and sacrifice that their pursuit demands.

PART II

The outlook for future development

10. Arab economic development: a conceptual framework

Part One of this book attempted to trace major developments in the Arab economies and in regional economic co-operation over the fifty years 1930–80. The discussion was of necessity backward-looking and generally descriptive, although at times it was analytical and sought to suggest lines of action in the future for the improvement of the region's economic performance. Part Two, on the other hand, will be forward-looking, and will therefore be mainly explorative and probing, in its attempt to assess broadly the outlook for future economic development.

Obviously the assessment cannot be undertaken in a vacuum. It will be rooted both in the experience of the past and in a certain conceptualization of what real development signifies, if it is to be meaningful for the Arab citizen and for Arab society as a whole. The experience of the past has been largely traced in the last few chapters, which indicated that, although the economic performance of the region has been erratic and unsatisfactory in many respects, there has been a generally commendable record of growth. It remains for us now to show more specifically and rigorously what development means, and what its attributes and content ought to be, if the drive for future development is to be soundly conceived, planned, and directed. This chapter therefore provides a conceptual framework which, it is hoped, will help to identify the attributes of comprehensive and meaningful development and, subsequently (in the next chapter), the major issues and tasks of future Arab development.

It may be helpful to recall in this connection that development was presented in Chapter 9 as a central objective of Arab society, along with security. These twin objectives were to be sought in a national as well as a regional context.*

*Throughout, the word 'national' is used to refer to a country or state, whereas the word 'regional' is used to refer to the whole Arab region. The differentiation is easier in Arabic, thanks to the use of the terms 'qutri' and 'qawmi', for national and regional respectively. The term 'qawmi' is used within the context of the belief in an Arab homeland embracing the whole Arab region, and the existence of an Arab nation and of Arab nationalism or 'qawmiah Arabiyyah'.

Furthermore, it was stated earlier that well-designed national and regional development interact closely and promote each other. In the same way development and security are interdependent: each is vital for the achievement of the other. The framework described below is based on this position.

The framework takes the form of a number of points of departure, which constitute the conceptual base for the discussion in the next chapter, and involves both the identification of the major issues and tasks of Arab economic development and the assessment of the outlook for this development in the remainder of the twentieth century. Indeed, neither the identification, nor the assessment, would be possible without the formulation of this framework and its concomitant points of depature; for the framework suggests what is expected of Arab economic development in the context of the present study, on what issues and tasks attention should be focused in the drive for development, and, finally, what outlook there is for development, given the specification laid down for it.

The discussion will now identify and present six points of departure:

1. It is essential, for optimum results in the pursuit of the objectives of Arab society, to go beyond the national approach to a regional approach. This must be done without losing sight of the particular endowments and problems of each country and the areas of differentiation this implies. Nevertheless, it is necessary to emphasize that the Arab countries, though numerous and spanning two continents, share a large number of vital interests and a common heritage, as well as certain fundamental hopes and expectations, in the economic, social, cultural, and political/security areas; they also seek to extend and enrich their shared experience of life.

2. Joint Arab action, of which economic action is one important facet, is more rewarding and effective in the service of the region's common interests than the mechanical accretion or addition of the efforts of individual countries. This is the more true the closer the co-operation becomes and the nearer it approaches harmonization of development strategies and policies and integration of a large part of infrastructure and

productive capacity in the individual countries, within an overall plan embodying an overall vision of the region's economy.

3. The correction of the process and pattern of Arab development, as these have taken shape over the past decades, must begin with a clear and profound understanding of the shortcomings of this development, in objectives as well as in content and structure. There is ample evidence of these shortcomings in the results achieved, once these are set against comprehensive development. What such development involves, and what are its requirements, will be the concern of the discussion below.

Part One indicated many of the major shortcomings, and attempted to provide evidence of them and to reveal their implications for Arab society, in the various areas or sectors examined. Chapter 11, the final chapter, will elaborate on the weaknesses and failings of the region's economy in the course of examining the issues and tasks of development.

But at this point it is essential to state that there is no consensus among those concerned with development, be they policy-makers or executives, intellectuals or analysts, with respect to the shortcomings of development. This is not only because the views of different people vary in their penetration and rigour but also because of the substantial confusion that surrounds the nature of development and all that it involves. While the economists are primarily responsible for the misconceptions causing the confusion, the responsibility must be shared by political decision-makers, planners, and those in charge of the interpretation and implementation of development programmes. Hence the need for a distinction between growth and development which is at the root of the confusion – a distinction that was clear to a few perceptive economists many generations ago, but which has since become blurred, as much of the economic literature in the first five or six decades of the current century shows.[71]

Although this is not the place for a theoretical discourse, it may be useful to recapitulate how the two concepts have come to be distinguished from each other. One prominent economist and social thinker made the sharp distinction more than seven decades ago. In his view, growth was a mere increase in national income (or real, national income per capita) which can take place within the 'circular flow' of the economy, given, that is, its social and political institutions and its technological capabilities and demographic realities. Development on the other hand, is growth of a size and continuity which cannot materialize without important changes occurring previously or concurrently in the technological, social, and political frameworks, in addition to the economic framework itself.[72]

The distinction has become much clearer and more specific, and more encompassing, since the early sixties by a number of economists, including some from the Third World. One recent work sums up as follows the specifications that must be satisfied before it can be said that development is occurring or has occurred:[73]

a. Rise in the level of economic performance, that is, rise in productivity and increase in the national product, within a sectoral pattern which is balanced as far as possible, and where manufacturing industry occupies a prominent position and is associated with the acquisition of the values of discipline, rationality, inventiveness, and scientific causality. Furthermore, the performance must be continually high, not a seasonal or accidental occurrence, and it must be the result of society's abilities and efforts, not of the activity of 'enclave sectors' that are weakly integrated with the national economy (like foreign plantations or foreign mining activities);
b. Provision of an expanded volume and improved quality of goods and services to satisfy the basic needs of the population – these needs to be understood in a dynamic context wherby the level or quantity of the needs rises and their coverage widens as they become increasingly satisfied; in other words, the satisfaction of one generation of needs leads to the emergence of another, more sophisticated generation;
c. Provision of distinctly wider opportunities for productive employment and the reduction of unemployment, whether open or disguised, and the mobilization of a very large proportion of manpower resources. This should be attempted both because of its social and human significance, and because of the purchasing power that employment can put in the hands of the population;
d. Correction of the pattern of income distribution within each of the Arab countries, by raising the income floor for the mass of the population, widening the base of ownership of productive assets, and reallocating the burden of development and of state services and

institutions in such a manner as to increase the absolute and relative contribution of those who have the financial ability to carry a larger share;

e. Parallel with income distribution at the national level, the narrowing of the 'development gap' among the Arab countries – that is, narrowing the wide differentials in economic capabilities and performance, which in turn would speed the advances in productivity and expand the national product in the less developed countries;
f. Evolving the capability of the social, cultural, and political environment so that it may provide the economy with the ideas, knowledge and skills, attitudes, and institutions necessary for the efficient operation of the economy, and for continuity in the improvement of the economy's performance;
g. Achievement of a wide measure of popular participation in the process of development and in the social, economic, and political decisions related to the formulation of development strategies and policies and the allocation and use of resources. The principle underlying this specification is that there can be no earnest and profound commitment to development and the tasks associated with it, without participation both in the design and the rewards of development; and, finally
h. Achieving the widest measure possible of collective (regional) self-reliance in development – not in the sense of isolationist autarky, but in the sense of the acquisition by the region as a whole of greater productive capability and its success in the mobilization of its human and material resources, and in the upgrading of the quality of these resources. Underlying and accompanying this specification is the need to improve the position of the Arabs in the world economy and its pattern of division of labour; the need to quickly and substantially remove the state of dependency on the advanced industrial countries and their TransNational Corporations, with all the exploitativeness, imbalance, and inefficiency that the dependency carries with it; and finally the desire and ability to contribute to the design and operation of the New International Economic Order, along with other regions of the Third World.

4. Regional development benefits from national development as it unfolds in each country, but the former is accelerated and becomes more firmly established, and more rational, once the Arab community as a whole resorts to co-ordination, complementarity, and integration in the development efforts of individual countries. The result goes far beyond the facilitation of trade, to encompass an organic meshing of the

productive capabilities (or of large parts of these) in the individual economies, guided by planning and programming in the Joint arab Economic Sector (to which reference was made in Chapter 9).

5. The achievement of an acceptable degree of national and regional security is an essential objective, worthy of effort and sacrifice, and that security requires a solid economic base which cannot be ensured without development that meets the specifications listed earlier. Likewise, the safeguarding of developmental gains calls for the achievement of security, in the face of Israeli settler colonialism, imperialist incursions, and continued threats. It is not necessary to emphasize that security in the present context is not restricted to the narrow confines of strategic/political/military security – important as this is – but extends to include the liberation of the Arabs whenever necessary from ignorance, poverty, disease, and internal insecurity; the liberation of Arab society from its dependency on foreign economic power and cultural domination; and the promotion of dynamism and creativeness in Arab society.

6. The identification of, and response to, the challenge of the major issues in development, and therefore the undertaking of the economic and social tasks associated with the response, cannot be achieved arbitrarily or haphazardly; it must be based on a prior conceptualization of what the Arab economy ought to become. This, in turn, can only derive from a conceptualization of what Arab society and the Arab homeland as a whole ought to strive to become with respect to its economic, political, social, and cultural features. Virtually all the discussion in this chapter is restricted to the economic sphere. But even so, the choice of options made, whether explicitly or implicitly, touches non-economic areas and concerns, and is value-based.

The choice of such far-reaching options needs no apology, as conventional and purely technical economics would suggest. Economics cannot remain value-free if it sets out to be concerned with development in its full sense and implications – that is, with the economic and social well-being, security, and dignity of man. It is therefore the issues and tasks associated with development in the service of such goals that will occupy us in the next chapter.

It remains to be added, finally, that the conceptual framework and the points of departure which constitute this framework give the impression that the discussion as a whole turns on regional development, or development in a regional context and from a regional angle of vision. This is deliberate: all along the present study has been concerned with the 'region's economy', and the latter term forms part of the title of the study. The reasoning behind this position is that, although there are twenty-one sovereign Arab states and therefore twenty-one economies involved, there is also an Arab experience of life, one important aspect of which is economic (other important aspects are historical, political, and cultural). Furthermore, the main tenet and message of the book is that it is beneficial and therefore necessary to intensify and strengthen regional economic complementarity and integration, not only for the region as a whole but also for its individual political and economic entities. The dominant force in the adoption of this position is that the march towards unity, in its political and economic content, is a cherished aspiration of the Arabs. The fact that this aspiration is not easy to translate into concrete, institutionalized reality constitutes a challenge which the Arabs are willing to face fully, even though it would require time and serious effort.

11. Major issues and tasks of Arab development

Before launching into a discussion of the major issues and tasks of Arab economic development as they appear to the observer and analyst three remarks may usefully be made. First that the process of development, as visualized in the conceptual framework formulated in Chapter 10, is necessarily very long and demanding, owing to the rich content of development and the stiff conditions that must be met before it can occur. This remark should silence any possible objection that the major issues and tasks examined further below are difficult to resolve and undertake; it should also warn all those concerned with the process of development not to expect spectacular results in a brief span of time.

The second remark refers to the last paragraph of Chapter 10, where it was admitted that the discussion proceeded within a regional context, as though it dealt with one economy for the Arab region. It is appropriate to state that the twenty-one Arab economies could, arguably, be treated not as one economy but as several homogeneous groups within the regional context. One such grouping could then be the oil-producing versus the non-oil countries; another grouping might be based on geographical location or on economic and social indicators. While such groupings are defensible, and might facilitate the analysis, it was thought that the advantages of a regional approach would outweigh the disadvantages, particularly if striking country-by-country deviations from the overall pattern were pointed out as the discussion proceeded. Furthermore, the region as a whole faces a number of common issues of major significance, and should – as a collectivity – undertake the tasks needed to resolve these issues, even though the intensity of the issues varies from one country to another.

The third introductory remark concerns the apparent overlap between the issues and the tasks discussed in the present chapter. The overlap is explainable and understandable:

what is regarded as a major issue to be resolved, constitutes a task to be undertaken if development is to be attempted. Indeed, the relationship between the issues and the tasks is the same as that between the two sides of a coin, which varies according to the angle of vision. In other words, every issue has a task attached to it or deriving from it. If this was not so, the identification of the issues, without an indication of the line of action to be taken in resolving them, would be a sterile academic exercise.

Ten major issues and tasks will be identified and discussed in the rest of this chapter.[74] A larger number could perhaps be listed and justified, but it is believed that the ones actually listed enjoy a high priority on grounds of significance, wide coverage, and strong relevance to the process of development.

1. Inadequacy of comprehensive conceptualization of development

It was only in the latter part of the sixties that a few national development plans began to reflect an overall conceptualization of development, involving the tracing of the broad features of the economy which it was desired to shape, the strategy for development, the system of priorities for investment, and the body of policies and programmes to translate the priorities into concrete realization. But at the regional level, such conceptualization remained totally absent until the last year of the seventies, when the Strategy for Joint Arab Economic Action was formulated, to be approved later in 1980.* Even with this strategy in hand, there is yet to be an approved plan for the Joint Arab Economic Sector, although the frame of such a plan was drawn up in 1980 by the Secretariat of the League of Arab States.

Needless to say, the conceptualization, and what it involves in the way of formulation of development objectives, strategies, priorities, policies, and major institutions, cannot be undertaken without a clear view of the economic system regarded as capable of optimizing the developmental effort which is to flow from the 'packet' that comprises the conceptualization and the other tasks following it. That the choice

*See Chapter 9 in this connection.

of system is not always discussed or mentioned in development plans and strategies, does not negate its relevance and urgency. Where such choice is not made explicitly, it is no doubt implicit in the policies and institutions opted for as guidelines and frameworks for economic effort. For present purposes, it is necessary only to indicate that the system chosen ought to assure the economy and society of efficiency in the allocation and use of resources; equity in the distribution of the burdens, sacrifices, and rewards of development; and rising economic/technological capability at home and far-reaching liberation from debilitating dependency on outside economic/political centres of power.

2. Inadequacy of the level of economic performance of a substantial part of the region

Another way of labelling this issue would be to say that underdevelopment is still a serious problem in much of the Arab region. This can be seen in the vast spread of poverty, disease, and illiteracy, not only in the six countries described as 'less-developed' in the literature, but also in large parts of the medium-income and even in some parts of the high-income countries. Poverty is of special importance here since it not only derives from low economic performance but in its turn also leads on to continued low performance, in a tight vicious circle.

The task that is called for by the issue of under-development is indeed overall development. But this is obviously too wide and loose a task as stated here, and greater specificity and narrower focus are required for its definition. To this end, we should first indicate that the level of performance can be considered to be rising when the volume of production rises, its spread over more goods and services widens, and the quality of products improves. And all this must take place alongside a rise in productivity of the various production inputs. The present focus on production, without reference to distribution, is justified on two grounds: first that there will later be occasion to turn to the question of distribution; second, the crucial nature of the volume of production: there can be little doubt that a small national product is unable to satisfy the stubstantial needs of a population, even if the pattern of distribution is made more egalitarian. Of course, this statement needs to be qualified quantitatively (by relating the volume of production to the size of population) if the terms 'small' or 'substantial' are to be meaningful, and the statement is to be rigorously convincing; but it is adequate for the purpose of a broad generalization.

It was suggested earlier that what is obviously a task necessary for the pursuit of a higher level of economic performance may none the less be very tough and demanding, by its very nature and the nature of the issue it is intended to resolve. This is because the task requires action on several fronts and at several levels, such as education and training, better exploration and utilization of resources, the acquisition of a serious work ethic and discipline, the formulation or adjustment of the appropriate economic strategies and policies, the expansion and improvement of physical infrastructure, the introduction of appropriate institutional changes in many fields – to name but some. These and other fronts of attack on the problem of underdevelopment provide a scope for action by the individual Arab countries, though in varying degrees of urgency, depending on the levels of performance already reached. They also provide scope for regional action. But, irrespective of where the burden of action falls, they all involve the need for substantive and substantial change if economic performance is to rise.

Most of the fronts of attack will receive consideration below; one, however, will occupy us here: physical infrastructure. It is fair to say that the Arab governments have shown great awareness of this field and its relevance to all aspects of economic activity. Relatively substantial investments have been made in infrastructure, particularly roads, ports, airports, and, to a lesser extent, telecommunications; and these have been given priority. However, corrective action is called for in three directions: (*a*) Expanding the infrastructure, particularly transport and communications, as it still leaves large parts of the Arab countries either entirely without facilities or poorly equipped, both in terms of quantity and of quality; (*b*) Upgrading the existing facilities, both because of normal wear and tear and because of obsolescence and fast change in technology. It should be noted here that the Arab countries need not attempt to keep pace with the fast and frequent changes of technology in the means of transport and communication, since these are quite often not necessary but undertaken under the impetus of the profit motive of large corporations in the advanced countries, which lure the Arab countries into the adoption of expensive technologies, regardless of the resultant waste in resources; and (*c*) Linking the national facilities wherever possible and necessary, in order to establish a well-equipped and efficient regional network. This would be of value for the emergence of a large regional market, the integration of the productive capabilities, and easier communication and movement between the peoples of the region's countries.

3. Inadequacy of the education and skills of manpower

This pressing major issue underlies virtually all the issues presented in this chapter. It is manifest in the high level of illiteracy – even its wider spread in absolute numbers over the last decade; in the inadequate ratios of school enrolment; in the high drop-out rate between the primary and secondary cycles of education; in the low ratio of enrolment in technical training; and in the disproportionately low rate of female participation in schooling; and, finally, apart from the quantitative shortcomings of education, the issue here examined manifests itself also in shortcomings associated with the content and methodology of education in the Arab region. Chapter 3 above presented some numerical and analytical evidence of the various aspects of the issue now under consideration, and we need not refer to this evidence again. But we must emphasize that the better education and training of manpower resources is of extreme urgency, since human beings are both the indispensable instrument of development and its ultimate beneficiaries. And, to the extent that education and training take into account the present and future needs of economic and social transformmation in society, manpower resources would all the better fulfil their dual function.

Raising the level of manpower capability is not just a matter of formal schooling and conventional course work and examinations. Well-rounded education must be accompanied by the promotion of science in its theoretical and applied forms. This involves the setting-up of the appropriate colleges and institutes, and research and experimentation facilities, in an economic/social/political climate that is both conducive and encouraging to research. But, above all, the underlying, insufficient interest in research must be corrected.

Quantitative information available shows that resources allotted to research in the Arab region are less than their counterpart (on the basis of size of national product) in other Third World regions, except in Africa south of the Sahara. Total outlay for research in the Arab region is currently estimated at less than one billion United States dollars a year. The extreme contrast can be found in the United States, where the 1980/1 federal budget allotted $36.1 billion for research and development, R & D, apart from allocations by state and local authorities and the private sector.[75] Serious concern with R & D would, moreover, express itself in the provision, by both the public and the private sectors, of laboratory, library, and other facilities; the institutional frameworks; a suitable atmosphere for work which would include primarily intellectual stimulation and freedom of thought, necessary for research and experimentation – in addition to reasonable financial incentives. Finally, unless the personnel in R & D are satisfied that their work is valued by society, and is considered both useful and usable, they will lose interest and fail to make a tangible contribution to economic life.

Obviously, this contribution is also related to the number of scientists, researchers, technicians, and skilled labourers, apart from the quality of their education and training. The Arab region has a slight numerical advantage over most other Third World regions in this respect. But the numbers are still well below the needs, if the Arab region is to intensify the utilization of trained personnel in the various areas of development and to devote substantially larger resources to R & D, with the object of becoming much more self-reliant. Lastly, the supply of scientific and technical personnel is further hit by the 'brain drain', from which the Arab region suffers acutely, particularly in the fields of engineering, medicine, and the areas of science relating to these, as well as in certain areas in the social sciences and the humanities, most notably economics. One specific area of expertise that is becoming necessary to modern economic life is computer science and related skills. But a substantial proportion of those newly trained in this area are seeking and finding employment abroad, mainly in the United States and Canada, but also in Western Europe.

Action to correct the general situation of inadequacy of manpower resources will have to be taken on several fronts. These include widening the quantitative base and improving the quality of education; providing the financial resources, facilities, and work climate for R & D; reducing the attraction of emigration for scientists and technicians by strengthening the 'pull factor' at home; and inculcating a feeling of social responsibility among the young in order to make them more eager to remain in the region and contribute to its progress. All these areas of corrective action, especially the last, require carefully thought-out policies and modalities and time to bring about positive results. A fact that only makes them all the more pressing as tasks to be undertaken and followed up.

4. Inadequate acquisition of appropriate technological capability

The Arab region faces a dual issue here: the failure to establish within the region sufficient technological capability to meet its needs, and the adoption of the wrong policies in the attempt to correct this. The first aspect concerns not only the absolute shortage of technological capability but also the under-utilization of the region's capability. The second is associated with the drive for the 'transfer of technology', which has been thought by some to be the answer. Both aspects received some consideration in Chapter 5; here we need to suggest some more specific areas in which action will be necessary if the issue is to be resolved satisfactorily.

One area in which such action could be taken at the national as well as the regional level, is in the setting-up of the appropriate institutions for research, experimentation, and training, in order to encourage the process of 'learning through doing'. This approach could usefully be supplemented by policies encouraging R & D activities; the stoppage of the brain drain, and possibly the reversal of the trend; and the identification of the needs and priorities of the region in the field of technology, in order to make the learning process match the body of needs better. In all this joint Arab action is necessary in the collection and sharing of information and co-ordination of policies. The resources for all R & D functions are estimated to amount to 1.5 per cent of GDP, and the aim should be to raise them to 3 per cent by 1990.[76]

As for the region's relations with the rest of the world, one aspect of a second policy area suggested by joint Arab action and based on the newly acquired economic strength of the region (thanks to its oil exports, its vast financial reserves, and the size of its commodity and services imports) must be stressed. This is the endeavour to adjust and improve the terms of purchase of capital goods and of expertise, or the hardware and software of technology, in order to speed the acquisition of technological capability by Arab manpower. Such a policy is particularly relevant to Arab dealings with Western industrial countries and their transnational corporations. The improvement in terms involves charging more reasonable prices for hardware and software; other matters are also involved, foremost among which is fuller and more effective co-operation in training Arab manpower and bringing it into close association with foreign experts in all the processes undertaken by the latter, beginning with the design and production of capital goods ordered, and their installation in the importing country, and ending with the running and management of the establishments for which the machines and equipment were ordered.

The socialist countries are particularly appropriate partners for technical co-operation for two reasons: the motive of private profit does not operate in their dealings, and their less complicated civilian technology is both more readily adaptable to the conditions of the Arab economies and easier to adopt; it is also easier to grasp than the vastly sophisticated technologies of the industrial market economies of the West. Furthermore, the socialist countries are not burdened by the reputation of the exploitative power of the transnational corporations.

Finally, with respect to relations with the outside world,

there is scope for co-operation among the regions of the Third World themselves. There are an increasing number of possibilities for mutual learning among the regions, and the possibilities have the advantage of involving technologies more germane to the endowments and cultures of the Third World regions. An equally significant feature is that the acquisition of these technologies represents a process of learning in, and by, the regions concerned.

A third policy area relates to institutional measures. The first component of these measures is the involvement of Arab design, consultancy, and management firms with much of the technical work which is now directed towards foreign firms. It is estimated that between 80 and 90 per cent of the contracts with foreign firms for the supply of software can be handled by Arab firms by the end of the eighties, if the right public policies and measures are adopted.

A second component is the setting-up of several industrial plants in the field of petrochemicals, since there is scope here for each plant to specialize in one major line of products, thanks to the large scale of production possible. Needless to say, the setting-up of the plants within the context suggested would involve close co-ordination among the Arab oil-exporting countries for the optimal geographical distribution of the plants, and the appropriate forms of integration to be adopted. The impact of these plants on the process of learning would be enormous.

Finally, an important institutional component involves the strengthening of Arab League bodies (or agencies associated with the League) engaged in industrial and technological activity, such as the Organization for Industrial Development, the Federation of Arab Engineers, and the Arab Centre for the Transfer and Development of Technology (which is yet to be formed, although the groundwork has been prepared).[77]

5. Slowness in the widening and diversification of the economies

As a whole, the Arab economies still depend heavily on a narrow range of products, in spite of the value attached to diversification and the efforts directed to that purpose. As indicated in Chapter 8, the sectoral structure of the economies, with very few exceptions, reveals imbalance and lopsidedness. But, whereas some decades ago it used to be agriculture which made the largest single contribution to GDP, today it is the hydrocarbon sector. Futhermore, the contribution of the latter sector still derives almost completely from the sale of crude oil, and to a much lesser extent liquefied gas, not from the sale of refined products or the products of petrochemical industries. In other words, there is extremely little diversification *within* the oil sector, even less than within the economies as a whole. The increasing pre-eminence of oil since 1973, has made the concentration even more serious than formerly, and calls for still greater efforts towards diversification, as we have shown in other chapters.

As stated earlier, the imbalance in the structure caused by the rise in importance and size of the oil sector has been accompanied by the sluggishness or stagnation of agriculture, the slowness of the process of industrialization, and the energy with which some less-productive service sectors have grown, in contrast to other service sectors that contribute greatly to development, such as transport and communication, and professional engineering and research services. Evidence of the sluggishness of agriculture is manifest in the zero growth rates of per capita production, the increasing importation of foodstuffs, or the draining-away from the countryside of many of its most energetic and ambitious inhabitants. We need not cite again here the modest contribution to GDP of manufacturing industry (already discussed in Chapter 5).

At this point, it is more appropriate to suggest some areas for which a definite policy is required. The first area is the energetic rehabilitation and promotion of agriculture. To this end, agrarian measures taken in the fifties, the sixties, and the early seventies should be re-examined so that their defects can be corrected. Foremost among these defects are the excessive centralization of these measures; the inadequacy and inefficiency of the institutional frameworks designed for agrarian reform, particularly in the technical, financing, and managerial areas; and the need for a more comprehensive and balanced understanding of the tenets and foundations of agrarian reform, in the sense that the expropriation and redistribution of land is not the only major aspect of this reform but must be supplemented by basic inputs such as cheap credit, extension services, improved seeds and stock, water, pesticides and insecticides, and fertilizers, and it should not stifle but promote individual enterprise and work incentives among the farmers. In addition to agrarian reform, attention should be paid to physical and social infrastructural facilities, storage facilities, and in general all those facilities that can make the countryside a more welcoming place to live and work in, and more rewarding for the amount of effort put into it.

The second area is industry. A number of areas in which Arab industrialization policies have gone wrong were enumerated in Chapter 5, and we need not cover the same ground again. Here it is sufficient to suggest that, fundamentally, this can be corrected by focusing on basic engineering industries, without which no industrial capability is competent to diffuse the industrial spirit and widen the industrial foundation. To this end, science and technology, and appropriate education and training, are called for. And underlying all this, there ought to be a proper, far-sighted, and wide-ranging concept of what industrialization involves, and what it should have as its central objectives. Finally, policy must address the task of introducing industrial processes into as many other sectors and activities as possible – particularly agriculture in the form of agro-industries, but also transport and communication, and construction. In other words, whenever possible, the inputs and the outputs of these sectors and activities should be processed in the Arab countries, instead of being imported, or exported, in crude or partly-manufactured or processed form.

The third area is the oil sector. There have been several references to this sector in the discussion, and there will be more, all within different contexts. The present context is the integration of the oil sector with the Arab economies and the economy of the region. It is with this special focus that the following paragraphs will be concerned.[78]

To establish how far and how effectively integration has proceeded, three questions have to be posed and answered. These are:

1. Where is the locus of decision-making for important

policies and issues relating to the oil sector, what is the content of this decision-making power, and what are its directions and orientations?

2. How significant is the contribution of the oil sector to the reservoir of financial resources in the oil countries, and how are the oil revenues used?
3. How has the oil sector promoted development, and what pattern and content of development has emerged in consequence?

The answers to these questions must scan the fifty-year period, 1930–80, which witnessed the rise in significance of the oil sector from zero to pre-eminence. This period can be broken into three sub-periods: the 1930s and 1940s, a phase of isolation; the 1950s and 1960s, a phase in which oil served as financial pump-primer; and the 1970s, which witnessed much greater integration of the oil sector with the national economies, and to some extent with the region's economy.

The 'phase of isolation' was one in which none of the criteria of effective integration were satisfied. Decision-making with respect to all significant issues (pricing, volume of production, direction of exports, extended exploration, downstream operations) was in the hands of the concessionary oil companies, in consort with their mother countries and inter-locking subsidiaries and associates. The second phase, in which oil served as financial pump-primer, witnessed only the initial emergence into prominence of the oil sector, with export revenues beginning to be significant, but not significant enough to permit the financing of ambitious development plans and programmes. This shortfall was due essentially to the fact that the locus of decision-making was still where it had been: outside the circle of national authority and effective sovereignty. So, once agin, integration was but beginning, and then only to the limited extent of increased revenues.

It was the third phase, the seventies, that witnessed substantial integration, manifest in three forms: the transfer of decision-making from the sphere of the concessionary companies to that of the national governments, the substantial widening of the flow of export revenues, and the intensified drive for development thanks to these revenues. It is extremely important to stress that it was only with the transfer to the national governments of the authority and the power to make major decisions that the other two criteria of integration were substantially satisfied.

However, the integration reported during the third phase still suffers from serious gaps, or is associated with consequences and implications that call for grave concern. There is room in this chapter for only a brief presentation of these:

(*a*) The revenue-generating role of the oil sector has three serious defects. The first is that the volume of revenues it is desired to obtain is associated with the fast depletion of oil, while most of the oil-exporting countries do not need all the revenues being generated. The second concerns the utilization of the revenues. The record of the seventies reveals areas of over-use and misuse of financial resources, whether for consumption or investment. The high and rising consumerism has serious implications, in that it uses up a disproportionately large part of GDP; it leads to the leakage of vast financial resources into imports, thus failing to encourage the diversification and expansion of national production; it creates patterns of behaviour which it will be very difficult to change later; and it deprives the region (and other Third World regions) of some resources that could be directed to investment. The third observation centres on the distribution of private income and wealth. The pattern of distribution reveals very large divergences between social groups, localities, and countries.

(*b*) The development-promoting role of the oil sector also betrays several gaps in the integration of this sector with the national economies. Probably the first and most serious of these is due to the inability of the drive for development to draw a large part of the labour supply of various oil-exporting countries into active engagement in development projects, and the rising dependence on expatriate labour force. A second gap is the slow pace of the acquisition of technological capability – indeed, the lengthening of the process – owing to the misguided, exaggerated policies of 'importation' of technology, to which reference has been made in earlier chapters. An associated point is the danger inherent in the extension of the influences and the strengthening of the grip of transnational corporations in the region. Finally, in the present context, the third gap is the unsoundness of five aspects of the pattern of the development emerging: (1) the slowness of the process of diversification of oil economies; (2) the sluggish expansion of the agricultural sector; (3) the insufficient care in the selection of industries to be developed; (4) the emergence of a large *rentier* class which flourishes on the fertility of its riches abroad in interest and dividends. The fact that this class invests at home does not invalidate the point that, in effect, it promotes the integration of a sizeable part of its country's resources with external economies, not with the national economies; and lastly (5) the disturbing rise in the level of dependency on the advanced industrial economies caused by the vast and increasing imports of consumer and capital goods, and of technological know-how.

(*c*) The oil sector has not yet been integrated substantially into the regional economy, or into the objectives and needs of regional complementarity and joint economic action. Although there have been substantial flows of manpower and of funds within the Arab region, these have been mainly haphazard, not submitting to a clear conceptualization of priorities in the light of agreed objectives; furthermore, the financial flows still fall sadly short of the needs and absorptive capacities of the capital-needy countries of the region. The matter of reserves in Western money markets is relevant here. These reserves are large and rising; they are expected to reach the level of $470 billion by 1985, on a conservative estimate. But they are also expected to lose over 38 per cent of their value (in terms of 1979 dollars) because of inflation, again on a conservative estimate.[79] The diversion into investment of part of the losses thus forecast would put into the development process, for both national and regional programmes and projects, substantial resources, which would be of decisive significance for economic performance and social well-being. In addition, such a diversion would promote the security of the region by strengthening its economic base.

6. Economic, geographical, and social imbalances

The first serious instance of imbalance to be discussed here is that between the supply of and the demand for labour. The gap between labour supply and manpower actively and gainfully employed is very large, as we have already seen. The failure of increasing economic activity and intensifying development work in the region to provide job opportunities for all those seeking them is a major issue that imposes urgent and heavy tasks on the decision-makers, in the public sector and the private sector alike.

These tasks do not fall solely and strictly in such areas as the choice of labour-intensive technologies and labour-intensive sectors and activities; they extend further to include education and training, the inculcation of more effective sensitivity to incentives and motivation, the organization of larger flows of manpower across national frontiers and the formulation of the appropriate policies for greater labour involvement and commitment, and the discouragement of the resort to non-Arab expatriate labour. Further afield, the tasks also include the revival of the countryside with a view to the reactivation of agriculture, and the provision of more and better work opportunities in the rural sector as broadly defined, the speeding of industrialization, and the encouragement of handicrafts. The pressures of mechanization and automation ought also to be examined, in order to establish a better balance between greater employment and cost-reduction.

It is necessary to point here to the fact that the first generation of Arab development plans, and many of the second generation, failed to direct adequate attention to the importance of the rise in the volume of employment as an objective. The oversight betrayed a serious economic and social lapse, and has had grave economic and social implications. These go beyond the damage which unemployment causes to the volume of production, and to purchasing power and welfare, to threaten stability and cohesiveness in society.

The second example of imbalance is that between the countryside and the urban centres. The development process over the five decades under examination in this book, but particularly in the post-war years 1945–80, has betrayed a sad neglect of the countryside. This neglect manifests itself in the relatively meagre attention given to agriculture and to rural society in the way of projects, funds, schools, health-care, and social and recreational facilities, despite the agrarian reform measures instituted in a number of countries. In contrast, the towns and cities, particularly the larger ones, have received an unduly large proportion of the resources and efforts of the society, although by no means enough to lead to remarkable development. The imbalance has led to large-scale demographic shifts which have resulted in the draining-away of an important component of the rural population and the overcrowding of the cities; a sub-optimal distribution of industrial capacity and facilities, and of social services; excessive concentration of central government and the weakening of local government; and generally a feeling of alienation and marginality among the rural population. The correction of these aspects of the imbalance constitutes a heavy and far-reaching task affecting several aspects of planning and action.

The third imbalance to consider is that among social groups within each country, manifest in the large, and widening, gaps in the possession of productive assets and in income distribution. While it is true that the floor of income has risen, it is also true that the ceiling of income has risen by very much more.[80] Similarly, the base of asset ownership may have widened – although this generalization requires careful research to establish it firmly – but at the same time there has been considerable concentration of ownership at the upper end of the scale, with excessively large fortunes being made that can be justified neither on grounds of equity or of merit, nor yet of economic exigency. At the same time, the system of taxation has failed glaringly in placing a proportionate demand on the wealth and income of the upper slices of wealth and income. The result is a very unjust distribution of the burdens of life and of social obligations.

It is important to indicate here that a large number of development plans, particularly those formulated in the fifties and the sixties, failed to pose the basic question: Who will be the *real* beneficiaries of the development envisaged? Although there were often references to social justice, welfare, and improvement in the level of living of the under-privileged social groups, these references remained in the realm of rhetoric, devoid of serious content or operational machinery. Consequently, the actual beneficiaries often turned out to be the powerful and the wealthy, again with very serious implications both for stability and social cohesiveness and for motivation and development.

To make the pattern of income distribution inside countries less glaringly uneven is extremely difficult owing to the vast unevenness already exhibited in several of the region's countries, and to the opposition of certain social forces, given the socio-economic philosophy prevailing and the existing socio-economic structures. Yet this task is probably more manageable than that relating to the correction of the fourth case of imbalance. This is the very wide divergence in the income per capita of the various countries of the region. The range of income across the region is very wide, from a low of $144 in 1979, to a high of $26,577, or a ratio of 1 : 185.[81]

Three observations must be made in connection with the case of imbalance under examination. The first is that the vast divergence in income per capita cannot be bridged effectively in the foreseeable future, given the logic of the arithmetic of the situation and the factor of oil revenues to which this divergence is attributable, even assuming a very moderate rate of growth in the oil-exporting countries and as high a rate as reasonable in the less-developed countries. The second is that the widening of the income gap between the low-income and the high-income economies is an observable fact common to all regions in the same historical phase of their economic experience.

The two qualifying observations necessitate the shifting of the focus from the income gap to the development gap, since the former is less significant than the latter, and at the same time less amenable to narrowing. It is therefore essential, even crucial, to concentrate on the correction of the developmental shortcomings of the less-developed countries. Indeed, a few of the medium-income countries of the region can be proved to have a distinctly superior developmental capability than the higher-income oil-exporting countries. The dual task required here is, therefore, the intensification of well-directed development effort in the countries suffering from low economic performance, along with the intensification of regional efforts involving co-operation and complementarity, with particular emphasis on the support and aid supplied by the more highly-developed and the capital-surplus countries to the less-developed, capital-short countries. This support and aid must aim at enabling the recipient countries to restructure their economies, and promote their economic performance, according to a soundly-conceived system of priorities.

The third observation is that it is easier to urge the intensification of financial, technical, and institutional aid than to effect it. To begin with, there is no regional sovereignty to put sufficient pressure on those capable of offering aid to make them actually offer it. Furthermore, the notions of interdependence among the region's countries, and between national and regional development, are not yet sufficiently entrenched and effective. Yet regional co-operation and complementarity are crucial to the narrowing of the development gap between countries. Moreover, co-operation will help the region achieve its dual collective objective of development and security, from which every country will emerge a net beneficiary. Only if every country is convinced that the rest of the region constitutes its *strategic economic depth* will sound co-operation and complementarity acquire the dimensions and the continuity that the task of correcting imbalance demands.

7. Inadequacy of natural resource policies

A major issue to be dealt with is the insufficient consideration and formulation of policies for the optimal exploitation and utilization of the region's natural resources. This applies alike to the mineral wealth of the region and to its land and water resources, possibly including scenery and climate as well. Exploration undertaken so far suggests that the region is not particularly richly endowed except with hydrocarbon and phosphate resources, and, to a lesser extent, sulphur, iron ore, and potash. Resources other than oil and gas abound in Iraq, Saudi Arabia, Jordan, Egypt, Tunisia, Algeria, Morocco, and Mauritania. The development of the techniques of remote sensing and of exploration may well widen the scope both with respect to minerals and to the countries concerned.

The exploitation and utilization of these resources call for wide-ranging and thorough surveys, exploration, and extraction. There is a great deal to be done in all three areas (except in so far as hydrocarbons are concerned). Once resources are found in accessible and commercial quantities, and are brought to the surface, two areas for which a specific policy is required have to be added: export and processing. The latter is of particular significance, inasmuch as oil and gas, though commercially exploited now for half a century, are still almost entirely exported in their crude form. The same applies to phosphates, the next largest mineral resource.

Oil resources call for special and more detailed attention, owing to their central role in national and regional development, their considerable revenues, and at the same time their crucial place in the world economy, which makes it necessary to add an international dimension to the analysis. This dimension itself underlines the link between national/regional and international considerations. Thus, oil policies in the seventies, when the centre of decision-making shifted to the Arab governments away from the concessionary companies, often reflected an ambivalence with respect to the relative weight of national/regional factors as against international factors. On occasion, the observer/analyst had to ask himself whether the sense of international responsibility had not outweighed national/regional responsibility in the determination of major policies and measures. These concern the volume of production and therefore the rate of depletion, prices and financial reserves in a world burdened with inflation, and the direction of trade in a situation in which oil is by far the greatest economic card in Arab hands (though one which is not played sufficiently well in the service of Arab interests).

It should be admitted that the questions of volume of

production and pricing are very complex, and that the components of the world economy are closely interdependent. This leaves the policy-maker unable to focus on his country or his region, without sufficient concern for the rest of the world. Nevertheless, the argument remains tenable that awareness of international responsibility should not dwarf the awareness of self-interest, but that the two should be woven together in a balanced texture.

To conclude this discussion, three guidelines are submitted as appropriate for use in the formulation of oil policies. The first is that oil stored in its natural reservoirs is better, from the Arab point of view, than oil produced and exported well in excess of national and regional needs and involving international responsibilities that the producers feel morally obliged to shoulder. The second is that oil in the ground will prove more useful to the Arabs in the future, not only because of the very high probability that its real price will not drop but rather rise over the years but, more pertinently, because the Arab region will have this strategic resource readily available for its own intensified industrialization, both as fuel and as industrial feedback. In this connection, the Arabs will be well advised not to submit to the attempts of intellectual blackmail to scare them into believing that future technologies of energy will render oil of little or no value. Every indication in hand points in the opposite direction.

The third guideline is that the awareness and the acceptance of international responsibility must be a two-way process. Thus, if the Arab oil producers are to continue extracting and exporting more oil than their national, regional, and international requirements call for, the industrial market economies, which are the major importers and consumers of Arab oil, ought to accept and fulfil their share of responsibility. This has three components: (*a*) facilitating the acquisition by the Arabs of technological capability, at reasonable prices and terms; (*b*) economic co-operation on equitable terms, in all spheres, but particularly in the building-up of a new international economic order characterized by specifications mutually agreed upon; and (*c*) providing effective support for the Arabs in their attempt to redress the injustice inflicted on them by Israel.

8. Low participation in, and commitment to development effort

One of the most serious ailments of Arab society and economic life, which impedes development from proceeding energetically, is the weakness of popular commitment to development plans and efforts, and the inadequate acceptance of the sacrifices and burdens, as well as the work discipline, called for by these plans and efforts. However, the weak commitment derives from the low participation allowed the population in the process of the determination of development objectives and priorities, in the creation of scope for dynamic initiatives, and in the enjoyment of an equitable share in the rewards of development. This whole issue can be summed up in the sentence *Where there is no participation, there is no commitment.*

It is obvious that raising the level of participation requires, first, the acceptance of the principle and practice of wide-ranging participation (which is essentially political, but also social and economic) by the various leaderships; secondly, the provision of the modalities and means of participation; and, finally, the education of the masses in the content of participation: what it involves in the way of commitment and duties, and what it promises by way of returns. The issue at the centre of the present discussion is the liberation of Arab men and women, and the exercise of their basic rights in an atmosphere of freedom, if society is to be expected to shoulder the demanding tasks of development.

Participation and commitment on the part of the population have another side. This is development orientation and commitment to development by the political leadership as well as the intellectual and economic leaderships. The region by and large suffers from the hesitation of these leaderships in their pursuit of comprehensive and profound development. While most of them have expressed great concern for development in the postwar years, this concern has not been adequately translated into objectives, strategies, plans, policies, and programmes aimed at serving the masses and promoting their well-being in security and dignity.

9. Sluggishness of the drive for regional economic co-operation and complementarity

The substance of the task required to tackle this issue is to move Arab economic co-operation to an advanced position, one of tight complementarity and integration, which will involve the restructuring of important parts of the Arab economies in such a manner as to lead to the meshing and interlocking of productive capacity. So far, co-operation has mainly involved the exchange of a, relatively, very small volume of goods and services, the joint financing of a number of projects, financial flows in aid, and the movement of manpower.

While these facets of co-operation are important in themselves and involve a large number of regional institutions and rather substantial capital, they do not on balance constitute integration of productive capacity in the various countries, except in a loose sense of the term. Viewed in its stricter sense, integration would go even beyond the organic linkage of productive facilities to embrace a common regional conceptualization of economic development and activity, a regional plan binding for the joint Arab economic sector at least, and decisions and policies taken and formulated jointly. This array of specifications must, of course, be supplemented by the appropriate legal and institutional frameworks.

The drive for complementarity has been blocked by several impediments, four of which deserve mention here: (*a*) the pressure of separatist vested interests, motivated by an incorrect assessment of the 'costs and returns' of integration; (*b*) the continued, even accelerated, growth of national tendencies (in the narrow country sense) at the expense of regional consciousness (in the sense of Arab supra-country identification and loyalty), in spite of the verbal support for complementarity given by Arab officialdom; (*c*) mutual mistrust and fear between the 'capitalist' and the 'socialist' systems in the region, even though this may be disguised outwardly; and (*d*) the ups and downs of Arab political life which are reflected in economic relations among countries.

These obstructions cannot be surmounted unless all leaderships, political, economic, and intellectual, are convinced that integration is of net benefit to all parties concerned; that it is crucial to the acceleration of national and regional development, and to the promotion of national and regional security; and that each country *needs* the rest of the region for its own development and strength. The rewards will reach into all sectors, activities, and capabilities. The main burden of the task of persuasion will necessarily fall on intellectuals and economists, 'opinion-makers', political parties, and syndical organizations. The educational drive that will be needed should aim alike at the general public and the political leaderships.

10. Excessive dependence on the advanced industrial economies

The dependence of the Arab economies on the advanced industrial market economies is generations old, but it seems to have intensified and acquired more disturbing overtones since the early seventies, when the Arab economies apparently acquired greater strength and a brighter promise of independence. The intensified dependence can be seen in a number of manifestations, which will be referred to briefly in the following discussion:

(*a*) The rise in the ratio of imports plus exports to GDP, as indicated in Chapter 7, and the impact of growing consumerism on the growth of imports;

(*b*) The grave implications of the steep rise in exports, which is entirely dependent on one major commodity, and the exposure and vulnerability of the Arab economy as a result of this monolithic structure. Similarly, the grave implications of the steep rise in imports for the region's purchasing power, which, by leaking outwards, thus supports the productive capacity of the supplying countries, rather than that of the importing countries;

(*c*) The intensification of dependence on foreign sources of the hardware and software of technology, in all stages and aspects of technology. This state has grave social and political implications, in addition to the techno/economic;

(*d*) Excessive and increasing dependence on foreign

money markets, which now host substantial Arab financial reserves and are destined to attract even more substantial reserves in the decade to come. We need not once again point to the losses incurred because of inflation and currency depreciation abroad, or to the constraining effect which the holding of the reserves in foreign markets has on the Arab power to take independent economic and political decisions;

(*e*) The precariousness of Arab food security, owing to increasing dependence on foreign suppliers of foodstuffs. Once again, dependence binds the ability to take independent action; and

(*f*) The 'cultural invasion' of foreign ideas, patterns of consumption, and values, even where certain aspects of the incursion are demonstrably harmful, not only to the Arab economies but also to Arab security and culture.

These and other manifestations of dependence persist, or are even intensified, partly because the Arabs have not seriously attempted to remove them, and partly because of the resistance of the powers behind the International Economic Order to the introduction of substantial change.

Action is therefore called for on two fronts. The first is the speeding-up and enriching of the process of self-reliance by the Arab region. As indicated earlier, this does not mean autarky or country-by-country self-sufficiency; it means a serious effort to increase regional economic and technological capability. Only this would permit co-operation and interdependence on the international level without exploitation of the weak by the strong, the developing by the developed. The second front is the building of the New International Economic Order, NIEO, which the Third World has for many years hoped and tried to achieve, in spite of strong resistance from the industrial world.

The specifications desired for the NIEO are that the changes and transformations it embodies should be substantial, not just marginal or 'cosmetic'. It is one of the tasks of Arab development, as of Third World development in general, to participate in the formulation of the image and substance of the New Order so that it may be characterized both by greater efficiency in the use of resources and by less waste and pollution; by greater concern with employment and the poor; greater justice in distribution of both the costs and returns of international economic relations; and by the ending of the marginal status of Third World regions and its replacement by their involvement and participation in the decisions and activities of the international economy.

The present chapter has attempted so far to identify the major issues of Arab economic development. It is appropriate to stress, once again, before we turn to the outlook for Arab economic development, that the issues, and the tasks deriving from them, are determined within the conceptualization of comprehensive and profound development, and the specification attached to it, as well as within the search for security along with development. This broad context has, in its turn, determined the approach to development and security, which is genuine and active Arab regional co-operation and complementarity, in addition to, alongside, and in interaction with, energetic efforts at the country level – provided of course that these efforts are soundly aligned with regional objectives and priorities and do not violate them.

No doubt the identification of the issues and tasks of Arab development is significant in itself; ideally, however, it ought to be accompanied by an identification of the strategies, policies, and instruments necessary for the undertaking of the assignments leading to the objectives of the Arab economy. If this complementary task is not attempted here, it is because the present book is not designed to comprise all aspects of the operational requirements of development. Nevertheless, five basic conditions that must be satisfied if the tasks stipulated are to be successfully undertaken will now be stated briefly, as a conclusion to the chapter and to the book as a whole:

1. The existence of the desire, and the will, for radical change in ideas and attitudes, which is called for by the nature and reach of the tasks discussed. This condition cannot be satisfied without far-reaching transformation of the socio-economic philosophies dominating the Arab

economy and society, in directions which imply an acceptance of the content of the tasks, and of the logic of their pursuit. In most instances the radical change thus necessitated will not be achieved easily and without struggle;

2. The existence of economic, intellectual, and political leaderships with a definite orientation towards development;
3. The mobilization of a broad popular base for the support of the drive for development. Such a base can be provided only if the Arab people have the opportunity for meaningful participation in the economic and political spheres. This condition is based on the conviction that where there is no broad and meaningful participation in the formulation of decisions, there will be no broad or firm commitment to them;
4. The existence of wide opportunities for education – an education which must be guided by social motives emphasizing the public good, alongside concern for personal welfare; and
5. The elaboration and implementation of integrative policies and measures involving the productive capacity and the manpower and financial resources of the region's countries, in a network of close co-operation designed to optimize economic performance and to promote security.

These conditions do not constitute a full, integrated system. They are rather an attempt to focus attention on the basic prerequisites that must be satisfied if the serious effort towards development is to achieve its objective in the years to come. It should be stressed that the objective in question is the emergence of an Arab society which conducts an energetic search for development, justice, freedom, and unity. These four pillars are crucial if the desired social structure is to rise and be sturdy; the neglect of any one of them will exact a heavy price in time, resources, expectations, and results, as the Arabs have discovered in their recent history.

Given the issues to be faced, and the tasks incumbent upon them, and given the necessary conditions for development, what is the outlook for this development? The answer cannot be attempted outside the context of the determining factors just referred to. Furthermore, to attempt an answer in terms of expected rates of growth would be to ignore our earlier warning not to confuse growth with development. We have therefore to keep comprehensive and profound development continuously within our sight while scanning the horizon for the outlook for future development.

Perhaps, in attempting an answer, it would be most useful to look at the Arab countries in three groupings. These would be the six less-developed countries (the two Yemens, Somalia, Djibouti, Sudan, and Mauritania), the seven oil-exporting countries (as defined earlier), and the other countries, which we can call the middle-income countries. The survey in Part One of the book and the analysis in Part Two suggest that the first group will continue to face very serious constraints on development at least until the end of the century, even assuming massive efforts by the countries themselves, and by their sisters in the two other groupings. This is because of the multiplicity of major issues burdening the less-developed countries, and the intractability of these issues, owing to both their dimensions and their intensity. Even if the first group were to achieve high rates of growth, they would still lack many of the attributes that permit movement into the range of development, at least within the two decades ahead of us in the twentieth century.

The oil-exporting countries, on the other hand, will be able to extend considerably their physical infrastructure as well as their industry and their financial sector, and to provide education opportunities and health-care services for all their citizens, and possibly for a large part of the expatriate population as well. But most of them will still only partly succeed in bringing about a substantial involvement of their labour supply in active productive employment. Furthermore, in most of these countries the productive capability will continue for many years to be very heavily dependent on expatriate manpower. This projection is based on the present situation and the trends which have led to it over the past two decades of expanded oil export and rising revenues – trends that are characterized by very low involvement by national manpower in technical work and a tendency to concentrate on administrative and executive responsibilities. Finally, there is a strong likelihood that most of the oil-exporting countries will concern themselves much more with the economic issues on which the present chapter has centred, rather than with such other issues as dependency, the income and wealth gap, or the restructuring of the international economic order.

The middle-income group of countries will probably move fastest in acquiring more of the capabilities and shouldering more of the tasks which promote comprehensive development, although they will still have a long way to go before they achieve a satisfactory level. This assessment is based first on the fact that this group already enjoys certain distinct advantages in performance and the other attributes of development; and, secondly, on the expectation that this base, coupled with the limitation of financial resources (in comparison with the group of oil-exporting countries), will provide a strong challenge which in turn will urge on the drive for development.

Finally, the outlook for regional development must also be explored. Here again, judging by the present situation after a third of a century of lukewarm efforts towards co-operation and complementarity, by the almost indifferent results achieved, and by the increasing power of separatist sentiment (irrespective of declarations to the contrary), it is fair to project very slow progress in the future. Thus, while there will be more and more joint projects undertaken, and more substantial flows of manpower and finance across national frontiers, there will be very slow movement towards a pre-designed pattern of regional development, submitting to a unified conceptualization, system of priorities, strategies, and plans and programmes. Furthermore, the dimensions of the joint activities undertaken, particularly with respect to the direction of considerable financial resources from the capital-surplus to the capital-short countries, will remain modest in relation to what is available, though substantial in absolute terms or relative to the decades preceding the seventies. Nevertheless whatever is achieved by way of intensified and planned co-operation and complementarity will be the result of a clearer appreciation by all parties concerned of the economic advantages involved and of the common dangers to which national and regional security continues to be exposed. In our estimate, this appreciation might take half a decade to achieve.

The exploration of the outlook ends on a rather gloomy but, in our view, realistic note. This in itself, however, is a challenge for more determined effort – an effort which could, given the satisfaction of the conditions stipulated earlier, invalidate the projections made. The rewards to be reaped from such an effort would be immense. This assertion is based on the reasoned conviction that an Arab society which is developing in the profound and genuine sense of the term, which has a high level of performance, which is just in distributing its opportunities and rewards, which is free and able to provide scope for its citizens to participate in decision-making, which protects its national and regional security and strives to liberate all occupied Arab land and to put muscle into the national will, is a society which would be worth all the sacrifice called for in its service. Such a society deserves to be at the centre of the hopes and energies of men and women striving for a better future.

Notes

1. See S. Kuznets, ed., *Income and Wealth*, Series V (Bowes and Bowes, London, 1955) for information on and examination of capital formation and investment during the period under discussion; also the Secretariat of the League of Nations, *The Course and Phases of the World Economic Depression*, Report presented to the Assembly of the League of Nations (Geneva, 1931); and the *World Economic Survey* series during the 1930s, produced by the Economic Intelligence Service of the League of Nations, Geneva. Only some Arab countries are covered by some of the economic surveys for the 1930s, notably Egypt, Palestine, Syria, and Lebanon, and Iraq in the Mashreq, in addition to the Maghreb countries. (The Mashreq includes Egypt and the Arab countries in Asia, while the Maghreb includes Libya, Tunisia, Algeria, and Morocco, all in North Africa.) However, none of the sources available contains a thoroughgoing examination of the impact of the Great Depression of the thirties on economic conditions in the Arab countries. See, for instance:

Samir Amin, *The Maghreb in the Modern World: Algeria, Tunisia, Morocco* (Penguin African Library, 1970);

A. E. Crouchley, *The Economic Development of Modern Egypt* (Longmans, London, 1938);

Charles Issawi, *Egypt: An Economic and Social Analysis* (Oxford University Press, 1947);

Sa'id B. Himadeh, ed., *The Economic Organization of Syria* (Beirut, 1936);

Sa'id B. Himadeh, *The Economic Organization of Iraq* (Beirut, 1938);

Sa'id B. Himadeh, *The Economic Organization of Palestine* (Beirut, 1938).

2. Galal A. Amin emphasizes this point in a recent book. See *The Mashreq and the West: An Examination of the Role of External Influences in the Evolution of the Arab Economic System and Arab Economic Relations* (Center for Arab Unity Studies, Beirut, 1979; in Arabic), especially pp. 32–5. (For Egypt, see Crouchley pp. 227 ff., for a discussion of the new policy of protection in 1930 and the industries that emerged as a result.)

3. The relative contribution to natural increase of a drop in mortality and a rise in fertility rates is not an easy matter to settle, as the behaviour of each of the two sets of rates differs in different phases of development. See Riad Tabbarah and Youssef Gemayel, 'Croissance des grandes villes arabes et migrations rurales', paper given at Colloque sur Les Espaces Sociaux de la Ville Arabe: Histoire et Mutations, Tunis, 12–18 March 1979. For a brief but clear analysis of the interaction of the complex of forces that influence the natural increase of population, see The World Bank, *World Development Report, 1980*, Ch. 5.

4. The World Bank bases its classification on Gross National Product, GNP, per capita. (Kuwait belongs to a special group labelled 'capital-surplus oil countries'.) See the World Bank, op. cit., Table 1 in Annex. For Bahrain, Oman, and United Arab Emirates, see United Nations Economic Commission for Western Asia (ECWA), *Demographic and Related Socio-Economic Data Sheets for Countries of the Economic Commission for Western Asia*, No. 2 (Beirut, 1978), country tables.

5. According to calculations made by three researchers collated together. See Charles Issawi, *Egypt at Mid-Century: An Economic Survey* (Oxford University Press, 1954), p. 58.

6. Food and Agriculture Organization (FAO), *1978 FAO Production Yearbook*, Vol. 32 (Rome, 1979), Table 1 for the recent data on land area and land use. For the earliest data presented in standardized form, see FAO, *Yearbook of Food and Agricultural Statistics 1950*, vol. IV, Part 1 (Washington D.C., 1951), Table 1.

7. Namely, the FAO 1950 *Yearbook* just cited. See 'Notes on the Tables', p. 257–8, for reservations about the data.

8. Area of cultivable land in the mid-seventies has been collated from various national sources, but without any attempt to standardize definitions or assumptions. The estimates cannot therefore be anything more than merely suggestive. See Yusif A. Sayigh, *The Economies of the Arab World: Development Since 1945* (Croom Helm, London, 1978), Table 14.2, p. 669.

9. N. M. Elgabaly, 'Agricultural Development and Land Management in Relation to Environment and Food Supply Needs in the ECWA Region', paper prepared for the United Nations Economic Commission for Western Asia, for Regional Seminar on Alternative Patterns of Development and Life Styles in Western Asia, 21–5 January 1980, Beirut, Lebanon (Paper No. E/ECWA/ENV/WG. 16/3, 13 December 1979). No such global comparison between potential and actual use of water is available to the writer for the Maghreb countries.

10. See Charles Issawi, *Egypt at Mid-Century*, pp. 99 and 100, and Mohammed Salman Hassan, *Economic Development of Iraq: Foreign Trade and Economic Development 1964–1958* (Sidon-Beirut, 1965; in Arabic), p. 29.

11. The data on storage and control capacity, as on hydroelectric generating capacity, are drawn from several sources, notably Issawi (just cited, pp. 104 and 145); Europa Publications, *The Middle East and North Africa, 1979–80* (London, 1980), country chapters; and Sayigh, op. cit., country chapters.

12. Sayigh, p. 670.

13. FAO 1950 *Yearbook*, Table 6.

14. The World Bank, *World Development Report, 1979*, Table 32, p. 72. For details of urbanization in individual countries for 1960 and 1975, see Table 20 (pp. 164–5) in Annex.

15. In addition to the sources of Table 4, see ECWA, Fathy Abu-Ainah, 'Primate Cities in the Arab World', paper submitted to Seminar on Population and Development in the ECWA Region, 18–30 November 1978, in Amman, Jordan, Table 5, p. 12. A glaring example of elephantine urban growth can be found in Cairo, whose population was 1,064,567 according to the 1927 census (see Crouchley, op. cit., p. 256), but rose to 8,539,000 by June 1979 (see Europa Publications, op. cit., p. 320), or from 7.5 to 21.1 per cent of total population which, in its turn, rose from 14.2m. to 40.5m.

16. FAO, *Production Yearbook 1973*, Table 5, and FAO, *1978 Production Yearbook*, Table 3.

17. According to a comparison undertaken by the writer for eighteeen Arab countries (excluding Mauritania, Somalia, and Djibouti) for the period 1960–79.

18. Data obtained directly from FAO Secretariat, Rome.

19. The discussion of agrarian (or land) reform, whether comprehensive or partial, is based on Sayigh, op. cit., the relevant country chapters.

20. For details, see the World bank, op. cit., Table 23 in Annex.

21. See Europa Publications, op. cit., country chapters, for specific information on universities.

22. For a discussion of the quality of education and a listing of the studies under reference, see Yusif A. Sayigh, *The Determinants of Arab Economic Development* (Croom Helm, London, 1978) pp. 110–16 and note 67 pp. 158–9. The writer also depended extensively on a large number of interviews in twelve Arab countries, and discussions with the Director and experts of UNESCO's

Regional Office for Education in the Arab Countries, Beirut.

23. Indeed, the plan of one country alone required some 496 thousand skilled labourers during the plan period, over and above those available in the country. At the same time, the aggregate enrolment in secondary technical schools in the whole Arab region was 615 thousand. In other words, one country alone could have absorbed 80 per cent of the aggregate, were it to proceed with its development work fully as planned.

24. Data for the early years are taken from the first regional statistical collection, which was compiled by the Jewish Agency for Palestine, Economic Research Institute. See its *Statistical Handbook of Middle Eastern Countries* (Jerusalem, 1945) p.p. 6 and 58.

25. Issawi, *Egypt at Mid-Century*, pp. 67 ff.

26. Data from Mohammed Omar Beshir, *Educational Development in the Sudan, 1898–1956* (Clarendon Press, Oxford, 1969).

27. Population estimates for the early 1930s (except for Syria and Lebanon) are quoted from League of Nations, *Statistical Yearbook* (already referred to), Table 2.

28. Data on Libya and Algeria come from Mohammed Munir Mursi, *General Education in the Arab Countries* (Cairo, 1974), pp. 268 and 130 respectively.

29. For both Transjordan and Iraq, see Roderic Matthews and Matta Akrawi, *Education in Arab Countries of the Near East* (Washington D.C., 1949).

30. All information comes from a very thorough study by J. A. Babikian entitled 'Civilization and Education in Syria and Lebanon' (Beirut, 1936; stencilled), pp. 199–216.

31. As told by a senior official of the Ministry of Education to the writer in February 1973.

32. Stephen Hemsley Longrigg, *Oil in the Middle East* (Oxford University Press, 3rd edn. 1968), pp. 66 and 67.

33. Yusif A. Sayigh, 'The Integration of the Oil Sector with the Arab Economies', paper given at the Oxford Energy Seminar held 1–12 September 1980, at St. Catherine's College, Oxford University. (Data obtained from Sayigh, *The Economies of the Arab World*, pp. 55, 37, 83, and 144, respectively.)

34. Information on production obtained from *Petroleum Economist*, January 1980. Revenue was calculated on the basis of a weighted average price of $19 per barrel for 1979. The average was derived from United States, Department of Energy, Energy Information Administration, *Weekly Petroleum Statistical Report*, 5 September 1980, p. 41.

35. Percentage calculated from data in *Petroleum Economist*, January 1980. For reserves, see *Oil and Gas Journal*, December 1979.

36. Data obtained from the annual report for 1978 of the Organization of Petroleum Exporting Countries (OPEC), and the Organization of Arab Petroleum Exporting Countries (OAPEC).

37. For installed capacity, see various issues of *Oil and Gas Journal*, 1979, but for capacity expected by 1985, see Abdelaziz Alwattari, *Oil Downstream: Opportunities, Limitations, Policies* (OAPEC, Kuwait, 1980).

38. According to Nizar al-Amin, 'The Significance of Oil Industries in the Arab Homeland' (OAPEC, Kuwait, 1979; in Arabic).

39. Data on oil consumption are collated from:

OAPEC, Statistical Services;

OPEC, *Statistical Bulletin*, 1979;

Country papers presented at the First Arab Energy Conference, sponsored by OAPEC and the Arab Fund for Economic and Social Development (AFESD), and held at Abu-Dhabi, UAE, March 1979.

40. The brief survey of manufacturing industry in 1930 and the early 1930s is

based mainly on country surveys, to several of which reference has already been made. See Notes 1, 10, and 24 above.

41. According to Samir Amin, the leading Arab researcher of the Maghreb economies, large-scale manufacturing industries were practically non-existent in the French-controlled Maghreb until 1945, and the industrial sector was growing at exceedingly low rates in 1930. See Amin, op. cit., pp. 43–4. Likewise, Charles F. Stewart (*The Economy of Moroco 1912–1962*, Harvard University Middle Eastern Monographs No. 12, 1964, p. 117), also found that a little over 5 per cent of capital in large industrial firms was Moroccan, and that the technical management was wholly French.

42. Foremost among these are:
Government of Palestine: *Census of Palestine, 1931*;
–*Statistical Abstract 1944*;
–*Statistical Abstract 1945*;
–*National Income of Palestine 1936*;
–*National Income of Palestine 1945*;
–*A Survey of Palestine* (3 vols., 1946).
Sa'id B Himadeh, *The Economic Organization of Palestine* (Beirut, 1938).

43. See Government of Palestine, *A Survey of Palestine*, Vol. I, Ch. 13, p. 499.

44. For value added, see Table 17. Data on employment in manufacturing industry are collated from several sources, but especially from country chapters in Sayigh, *Economies of the Arab World*. It is worth observing that manufacturing, according to the World Bank, *World Development Report, 1980*, Table 3 in Annex, excludes electricity, gas, and water. Nevertheless, value added in the sector for Egypt and Syria is much higher than indicated in the Arab Fund Tables in Table 17 (25 and 21 per cent respectively), and about equal for the other countries listed in the text.

45. The clearest identification of the region's shortcomings with respect to policies and measures relating to technology, and the suggestion of corrective action, can be found in the writings of A. B. Zahlan. See, for instance, A. B. Zahlan, ed., *Technology Transfer and Change in the Arab World* (Pergamon, London, 1978), and A. B. Zahlan, *Science and Science Policy in the Arab World* (Croom Helm, London, 1980). See also League of Arab States, Directorate-General of Economic Affairs, 'Joint Arab Action with Respect to the Acquisition of Technological Capability' (July, 1980; in Arabic).

46. The rest of the discussion on manufacturing industry in the present chapter draws heavily on, and follows the structure of, an essay by Burhan Dajani entitled 'The Strategies of Industrial Development in the Arab States', in *Arab Economic Report* (General Union of Chambers of Commerce, Industry, and Agriculture for Arab Countries; Beirut, December 1979; in Arabic).

47. See, in this connection, a well-known work by Clark Kerr, John T. Dunlop, Frederick Harbison, and Charles A. Myers, *Industrialism and Industrial Man: The Problems of Labor and Management in Economic Growth* (Harvard University Press, Cambridge, Mass., 1960).

48. All the data on banks, except where otherwise noted, come from Union of Arab Banks, *The Directory of Arab Banks* (Beirut, not dated, but known to refer to the very late 1970s; in Arabic). This is a very thorough, large volume covering the whole Arab region in detail. For further information on the thirties, see the relevant parts of the sources listed in Note 1 above.

49. There are many essays and studies on Bank Misr. The information referred to in the text draws on the works by Crouchley and Issawi referred to earlier.

50. See an article entitled 'Arab Banks Grow' in *Business Week*, 6 October 1980, pp. 70–84. The listing of top banks is from p. 73.

51. Statement based on the reference sources listed in Note 1 above. For the Maghreb, see Samir Amin, op. cit., pp. 48 ff.

52. Data are for 1979, except for United Arab Emirates, Qatar, Oman, Yemen Arab Republic, Sudan, Libya, Mauritania, and Somalia, where budget provisions were available for 1978 only at the time of writing. A general increase of 10 per cent was (arbitrarily) applied to adjust the estimates upwards to 1979. Data collated from Europa Publications, op. cit.; *International Financial Statistics* (*IFS*,) September 1980; and the General Union . . . . op. cit. [Note 46 above], country chapters.

53. According to the Arab Fund (AFESD) National Account Country Tables, to which reference has been made, gross fixed capital formation for 1979 stood at $87,506 million for the Arab countries, except for Djibouti. It should be stated here that the total of aggregate consumption in the Arab region ($160 billion) and aggregated gross investment ($87.5 billion) falls short by $53 billion of aggregate GDP ($300 billion). This 'discrepancy' constitutes savings that are not invested inside the region but leak outside for overseas placement.

54. Data for the 1930s come from various sources cited in Note 1, and for 1979 from AFESD National Account Country Tables.

55. A word of explanation is called for here. It was stated in Chapter 4 that the market value of oil production for the Arab countries combined was $160 billion. This was based on a weighted average price for the total volume of production (see Note 34 above). However, the value of oil exports was lower, since local consumption is assumed to have accounted for about 7 per cent of total production, as against 6 per cent for 1978. (Two other factors should qualify the value of exports: the value of the exports of liquefied gas, and the average price of crude sales in the spot market, neither of which is available.)

Assuming that consumption is 7 per cent of total production, the market value of total crude production exported would be $148.8 billion. These exports would thus constitute 87.9 per cent of total exports. The proportion would be much higher if commodity exports alone (excluding services) were used as the base for calculation, and gas exports were added to crude exports.

56. Foreign trade data (totals, composition, geographical distribution) are based on sources listed in Note 1 above, or calculated therefrom.

57. The current account of the balance of payments includes other items than those in Table 16, but it was not felt necessary, for present purposes, to go beyond the major items mentioned in the Table.

58. For 1970 and 1978, see AFESD, *Study of the Developmental Achievements of the Arab Homeland in the Seventies, and the Outlook for the Eighties* (Kuwait, April 1980; in Arabic), p. 24, and Table 2 in Appendix 3. The percentage for 1979 is calculated by the writer.

59. Aggregated from the Arab Fund National Account Country Tables.

60. Fadhil al Chalabi, 'OPEC and the Non-Oil Developing Countries', paper given by the Deputy Secretary-General of OPEC at the Oxford Energy Seminar, 1–12 September 1980. This paper covered data on aid for 1974 to 1978; data for 1979 are quoted in the World Bank *World Development Report, 1980*, Table 16 (p. 140–1) in Annex. It is worth noting, however, that aid is reported at a lower level in the *World Development Report* for 1975 to 1978, both for OECD and for OPEC countries.

61. For estimates for the five countries enumerated for 1930 and the thirties, see the relevant sources in Notes 1 and 42 above.

62. See Sayigh, the appropriate chapters in *The Economies of the Arab World* for the early national accounts of the countries cited, and the pioneering work undertaken in this respect by a few Arab scholars.

63. The World Bank, *World Development Report, 1980*, Tables 1 and 23 in Annex.

64. Ibid., Table 22 in Annex.

65. For the proportion of investment over the thirty years 1945–75, see Sayigh, *Economies of the Arab World*, Ch. 14. The statement regarding 1979 is based on Table 16 and on AFESD National Account Country Tables.

66. In this connection, see Yusif A. Sayigh, 'The Economic, Social, and Environmental Implications for the ECWA Region of Present and Future Trends in International Relations', paper prepared for the United Nations Economic Commission for Western Asia, for Regional Seminar on Alternative Patterns of Development and Life Styles in Western Asia, 21–5 January 1980, Beirut, Lebanon. (Paper No. E/ECWA/ENV/WG. 16/2, 12 December 1980.)

67. See Yusif, A. Sayigh, 'The Social Cost of Oil Revenues', paper given at the First Arab Energy Conference held in March 1979 (already referred to). See also Arab Fund for Economic and Social Development, and Organization of Arab Petroleum Exporting Countries, *Energy in the Arab World* (Kuwait, 1980; 3 vols.), Vol. 1, pp. 323–41. An Arabic version of the paper appeared in *Al Mustaqbal Al Arabi* (The Arab Future), a monthly published by the Center for Arab Unity Studies in Beirut, No. 8, July 1979, pp. 23–33.

68. The historial narrative in this chapter, and the discussion of the avenues and forms of co-operation, are adapted from Yusif A. Sayigh, *Economies of the Arab World*, pp. 691–710. In a few instances direct quotations are made, as indicated in the text.

69. For a fuller discussion of these approaches to co-operation and of its other aspects, see Yusif A. Sayigh, 'Arab Economic Integration: The Alibi of Sovereignty', paper given at the XIth Congress of the Arab-American University Graduates held in Minneapolis, Minn., October 1978. (An Arabic version of the paper appeared in *Al Mustaqbal Al Arabi*, No. 6, March 1979, pp. 23–41.)

70. The writer draws heavily here on his personal connection with the Strategy for Joint Arab Economic Action, and the thirty studies prepared around it. He was privileged to have served as a member of the Strategy Committee (the 'Committee of Twenty' referred to in the text), and to have been asked in 1979 by the Assistant Secretary-General of the League of Arab States to draw up a strategy. This he did, assisted by Dr Mahmoud Abdul-Fadheel and Dr George Corm. Early in 1980, he was also asked by the Secretary-General to co-ordinate and edit all the studies prepared around the strategy, to be submitted to the Council of Arab Heads of State (the 'Arab Summit'), held in November 1980, in Amman, and to write the principal paper for the Summit. (Document No. 1/S.)

71. Adam Smith, in his *Wealth of Nations* of 1760, was well aware of the distinction between growth and development, an awareness which is to his credit when compared with subsequent confusion by the multitude of economists who followed him over the generations. Although he did not use the terms as we use them today, it is evident from his writings that he understood the true nature of development.

72. Joseph A. Schumpeter made this distinction clearly and convincingly in 1909, when his book *The Theory of Economic Development* first appeared in German.

73. Yusif A. Sayigh, *The Determinants of Arab Economic Development*, Ch. 1. The 'points of departure' are also systematically presented in the Strategy of Joint Arab Economic Action document (referred to above). See League of Arab States, Directorate-General of Economic Affairs, Document No. 5/1/S, submitted to the Arab Summit in November 1980, in Amman.

74. Chapter 11 is partly an adaptation from, and an expansion of, a paper by

the writer entitled 'Arab Economic Tasks Till the End of the Twentieth Century'. (See *Oil and Arab Cooperation*, a quarterly published by OAPEC in Kuwait, in Arabic with English summaries; Vol. 5, No. 9, 1979, pp. 9–31.)

75. As reported in the *New York Times*, 15 September 1980, p. A 23.

76. League of Arab States, Directorate-General of Economic Affairs, 'Joint Arab Action with respect to the Acquisition of Technological Capability' (July 1980; in Arabic).

77. Ibid.

78. This discussion is based on Yusif A. Sayigh, 'The Integration of the Oil Sector with the Arab Economies', already referred to. (See Note 33 above.)

79. Data from League of Arab States, Directorate-General of Economic Affairs, 'Arab Reserves Abroad' (July 1980; in Arabic).

80. For income distribution, see Ali Sadiq, 'Some Economic Features of the Arab World', in *Oil and Arab Cooperation*, Vol. 4, No. 4, pp. 162–80.

81. See the population and GDP data for 1979 for Somalia and the United Arab Emirates in Tables 1 and 17 in Part One of the book.